Winter

*For Sheila and Debbie
with love*

Winter

Resources for November, December and January

including Remembrance, All Saints', Advent, Christmas, New Year and Epiphany

Ruth Burgess

wild goose publications www.ionabooks.com

Contents of book © individual contributors
Compilation © 2016 Ruth Burgess

First published 2016 by
Wild Goose Publications
Suite 9, Fairfield, 1048 Govan Road, Glasgow G51 4XS, Scotland
A division of Iona Community Trading CIC
Limited Company Reg. No. SC156678
www.ionabooks.com

ISBN 978-1-84952-509-1

Cover photograph © Jens Zieschank from Pixabay

We gratefully acknowledge the contribution of the Drummond Trust,
3 Pitt Terrace, Stirling, towards the publication of this book

All rights reserved. Apart from the circumstances described below relating to non-commercial use, no part of this publication may be reproduced in any form or by any means, including photocopying or any information storage or retrieval system, without written permission from the publisher via PLSclear.com.

Non-commercial use: The material in this book may be used non-commercially for worship and group work without written permission from the publisher. Please make full acknowledgement of the source along with our website address (www.ionabooks.com). If photocopies of sections are made, please report usage to CLA or other copyright organisation.

Ruth Burgess has asserted her right in accordance with the Copyright, Designs and Patents Act, 1988, to be identified as the author of this compilation
and the individual contributors have asserted their rights to be identified
as authors of their contributions.

Overseas distribution
Australia: Willow Connection Pty Ltd, 1/13 Kell Mather Drive,
Lennox Head NSW 2478
New Zealand: Pleroma, Higginson Street, Otane 4170, Central Hawkes Bay

Printed in the UK by Page Bros (Norwich) Ltd

Contents

Winter in November   17

Souls and saints   25

Remembrance   45

Thanksgiving Thursday and Black Friday   53

Christ the King/The reign of God   61

Advent   75

Watching and waiting   93

Blue Christmas   107

Winter in December   129

Christingle   145

Early Christmas Eve   163

Watchnight   181

Christmas Day   197

The Christmas story   211

Mary and Joseph   221

Shepherds and angels   237

Holy Innocents and Holy Family   253

New Year   261

Epiphany   281

Homelessness Sunday   297

Winter in January   305

The baptism of Jesus   325

Prayers for Christian unity   337

Blessings and sendings   345

Contents in detail

Introduction   15

Winter in November   17

- ✞ A prayer for growth in winter   18
- ✱ The Penmon robin   18
- ✱ Winter haiku   19
- ✱ A bit of a blow   20
- ▦ The day of the storm   20
- ⦅◎⦆ Remind me: a prayer during winter's storms   21
- ♪ A blink of sun   22
- ▦ Like November   23
- ✱ Red lantern of light   24

Souls and saints   25

- ▦ We are part of each other   26
- ▦ Really, God?   26
- ▦ Reflection for All Souls' Day   27
- ☒ A liturgy of death and new life –
  St Winefride (Gwenfrewi), 3rd November   30
- ♪ In steps of saints   34
- ✞ We give thanks   35
- ⦅◎⦆ Prayers for an All Saints' Communion   36
- ☒ St Lucy's Day (December 13)   38
- ✞ A prayer for All Saints'   39
- ▦ What I miss when I am missing you   40
- ✣ Saints alive   41
- ▦ They're all around us   42

Remembrance   45

- ⦅◎⦆ From the darkness of death   46
- ☒ They shall not grow old   46
- ✞ We commend to you   48

Winter 7

- ((○)) A response for Remembrance Day   49
- ✞ Loving God   49
- ▦ The ordinary people   50
- ✞ Seeking the ways of peace   50
- ✞ Let us go from this place   51

Thanksgiving Thursday and Black Friday   53

- ▦ Another leaf in the table   54
- ▦ Thanksgiving   55
- ✞ Thank you   56
- ✜ The mall is my shepherd   57
- ✞ Prayer for Black Friday   57
- ▦ Buy Nothing Day   58
- ▦ Black Friday!   59

Christ the King/The reign of God   61

- ▦ You I could follow   62
- ((○)) From seed to shoot   63
- 🎭 The Christian year   64
- ✍ Christ reigns   66
- ((○)) Opening responses   68
- ✞ Closing prayer   68
- 🎭 The king and the castle   69
- ✍ Waiting for a God of   72
- ✞ A sending   74

Advent   75

- ✱ Poem for Advent   76
- ▦ St Nicholas Day (December 6th)   76
- ▦ Just when   77
- ✍ Advent wreath ceremony   78
- ▦ Gladness   80
- ▦ God approaches   81
- ▦ For such mornings as this   82

Key to symbols	
✞	Prayer
✜	Biblical reflection
✍	Liturgy
♪	Song
🕮	Story
🎭	Script
♥	Meditation
▦	Reflection
✱	Poem
((○))	Responsive prayer
✓	Affirmation

✝ Intercessions for Advent   83
✝ Prayer of approach and adoration   84
🏛 Gaudete Sunday   85
♪ A song for Gaudete Sunday   86
✝ God in the dark   87
📢 Advent call   87
🎭 Responses and prayers for the Sunday before Christmas   88
♪ As we wait   90
📢 Be with us, God   91

Watching and waiting   93

♥ Be still (Psalm 37)   94
🏛 Watching and waiting   94
🏛 Winter's wisdom (an Advent invitation to foolish waiting)   96
✝ Advent again   96
♥ Know that I am God (Psalm 46)   97
✝ The light time and the dark time   97
🏛 The bogey-god   98
♥ The Spirit broods   99
✝ In Advent we wait for you   100
🏛 Evening service   100
✝ Hoping and yearning   101
✝ Bearers of hope   102
🏛 We come expecting nothing   102
📢 For you we wait   104
📢 We will watch and we will wait   104
🎭 We are waiting   105

Blue Christmas   107

🎭 Bring it all to me (a service for the longest night)   108
🏛 Homecoming   113
✝ The longest night   114
✝ Until the light comes again   115
✣ Companion   115

♪ Bring your peace, Lord   116
☒ A liturgy of remembering   118
☒ Time to remember   123
▦ Christmas doesn't work for everyone   128

Winter in December   129

✞ A thanksgiving for winter   130
✺ Solstice   131
♥ Seeking silence   132
▦ The heavens declare   132
✺ Winter in Dunblane   133
((◉)) Midwinter on Ulva ('We have come, following a star')   134
✺ Long for home   135
▦ Longest night   136
✺ When the snow falls deep   137
✺ Winter praises   138
✺ Winter shore walk   139
▦ The light shines   140
▦ Kinharvie walk   140
✢ The sense of winter   142
((◉)) Winter prayers   143
♪ The Lord of the winds   144
✺ Stars   144

Christingle   145

((◉)) Three sets of opening responses   146
✞ A prayer for a Christingle service   147
☒ A story with dressing up   148
☒ A story with actions and noise   151
☒ Litany of the Christingle   154
🎭 Leftovers   161
✞ Benediction (for when the Christingle service is held on Christmas Eve)   162

Key to symbols	
✞	Prayer
✢	Biblical reflection
☒	Liturgy
♪	Song
🕮	Story
🎭	Script
♥	Meditation
▦	Reflection
✺	Poem
((◉))	Responsive prayer
✓	Affirmation

Early Christmas Eve 163

- 🔊 There was no room   164
- ✶ Christmas Eve   164
- ✝ Child of Bethlehem   165
- 🍃 Mary and Joseph at Capstone Farm   166
- 🍃 Yusuf was bored   167
- 🔊 Lord Jesus, hear our prayer   170
- ✝ Earth-dwelling God   171
- ♪ Oh, that we were there   172
- 🎭 The Angel Tam   173
- 🎭 Are you ready? A Christmas Eve play   176
- ✝ God who loves to be with us   179
- ✝ A crib prayer   179
- 🍃 Christmas Eve tonight   180

Watchnight 181

- ♥ He walked alone on Christmas Eve   182
- ♪ All this night   184
- 🎸 The bothy   186
- ✶ Christmas came simply   187
- 🎭 It was dark   188
- 🎸 In the darkness   190
- ✝ A Christmas blessing   191
- ✝ A prayer for others   192
- 🎸 Hope came   193
- ✝ Light, to crumple up the darkness   195

Christmas Day 197

- ✝ God in a manger   198
- 🎭 No and yes   198
- ✶ In memoriam   200
- ✶ Aren't primary-school Nativity plays embarrassing?   201
- ✝ The song of the angels   201
- ♪ The Lord of life   202

✓ We believe in Christmas   206
✞ Bidding prayers   208
✞ A Christmas Day blessing   209
♪ Look, Lord, said the angels   210

The Christmas story   211

🎭 Luke and Matthew (for two voices)   212
🎭 The householder's story   215
🎭 I can talk now   216
▦ The two songs   218
✣ Elizabeth watches the hoopoes   219

Mary and Joseph   221

♪ To be a good man   222
🎭 Advice from uncle   223
🎭 A wee dose of reality   224
▦ Saying yes   226
✣ Hello, bump   226
🎭 God delivers: a dialogue between Joseph and a friend   228
♪ My soul magnifies the Lord   230
🎭 'Mary – he's beautiful'   231
🎭 Our story   232
✣ Advent thoughts from Our Lady in old age   234

Shepherds and angels   237

🎭 Wash night: a shepherds and angels drama   238
▦ Angels are special   240
♪ Come and sit   241
▦ Angels say   242
▦ A shepherd's story   242
🎭 Something aaamazing (for three voices)   243
🗣 The story of Josh and his sheep   246
♪ Glory to a child   252

Key to symbols

✞ Prayer
✣ Biblical reflection
∅ Liturgy
♪ Song
🗣 Story
🎭 Script
♥ Meditation
▦ Reflection
🗡 Poem
((○)) Responsive prayer
✓ Affirmation

Winter

Holy Innocents and Holy Family   253

- 🎴 Little boy in Bethlehem   254
- 🎵 Walking to Bethlehem   254
- 🎭 Night flight   256
- 🐴 Donkey monologue   258
- 🎴 To Egypt   260

New Year   261

- 🎵 As the old year passes   262
- 🎴 Got your list done?   263
- ✝ New year – new me   264
- ✝ Again we come   264
- 🎵 Change me, God   266
- ⊘ A liturgy of hopeful brokenness   270
- ✝ Bring us bright God   272
- ✝ God of our past   272
- 🎴 Covenant challenge   273
- 🎴 Covenant of love   274
- 🎴 If I had   274
- ✝ Blessed are you   275
- 🎴 The 'in-between' Sunday   276
- 🎴 Travelling with God   276
- ✝ God our provider   277
- ✝ Fresh is the morning   278
- ✝ Dancing in the rain   279

Epiphany   281

- 🎵 A star for our journey   282
- ✢ Star of wonder   282
- 🎴 We all have gifts   284
- 🎴 Mary remembers the visitors   284
- 🎵 We use our gifts for God   285
- 🎭 We are   286
- ✢ Wise   288

♪ A bright light is shining   289
✝ Strangers at the door bringing gifts   290
▦ The wise of old   290
✝ Those first visitors   291
☻ WOW!   292
✝ New roads   295

Homelessness Sunday   297

✝ We belong to God   298
✷ Walking by the homeless   298
((()) May our hearts and minds be open   299
♪ Dilemmas   300

Winter in January   305

✝ As the sun revives   306
✝ God of ever-new beginnings   306
✓ A litany of hope   307
✷ Angel in the dump   308
✷ That name   309
♪ Lord of the seasons   310
📖 At the pantomime   314
✷ January dawn   315
✷ Winter walk on Hod Hill   316
📖 The first time   316
℧ A communion liturgy   320
✷ January 28th   322
✝ Winter hope   323
✝ Turning the sod   324

The baptism of Jesus   325

☻ He scared me   326
✣ Am I ready?   327
☻ What did it for me   328
✝ To live out our baptism promise   330

Key to symbols	
✝	Prayer
✣	Biblical reflection
℧	Liturgy
♪	Song
📖	Story
☻	Script
♥	Meditation
▦	Reflection
✷	Poem
((())	Responsive prayer
✓	Affirmation

- ▦ Pirate Jesus   331
- ⚘ In this spirit we baptise you   332
- ♫ Look what you can be   333

Prayers for Christian unity   337

- ⦅⦆ An opening prayer   338
- ✞ We ask for courage   339
- ✞ Our united service   340
- ♫ Give us grace   341
- ✞ Bidding prayers   342
- ✞ A prayer for Christian unity   343

Blessings and sendings   345

- ✞ God's blessing be ours   346
- ✞ In our heart a dream   346
- ✞ A winter blessing   346
- ✞ A blessing from Bethlehem   347
- ✞ A good work   347
- ✞ May God salt the path before you   347
- ⦅⦆ When   348
- ♫ Praying the day through   348
- ✞ Time for rest   349
- ✞ Bless you   349
- ✞ This long night   350

Sources and acknowledgements   351
About the authors   352

Key to symbols

✞	Prayer
✣	Biblical reflection
⚘	Liturgy
♫	Song
🖎	Story
🎭	Script
♥	Meditation
▦	Reflection
✽	Poem
⦅⦆	Responsive prayer
✓	Affirmation

Introduction

Winter is a liturgical resource book that covers the months of November, December and January. It includes the major Christian festivals of All Saints', Advent, Christmas and Epiphany, as well as material for Remembrance, Blue Christmas, Christingle, New Year and Christian Unity.

It's twelve years since I first began compiling and editing a series of resource books that covered the liturgical year, and it's been good to begin again, in a slightly different format, with *Winter*.

I've defined each season by the month that contains the solstice or equinox and the month either side of it. Given the quality and amount of material that was contributed to this book, completing the series in due course, with *Spring*, *Summer* and *Autumn*, should be a pleasure and a delight.

Thank you to all the contributors for their rich and imaginative material that I have been privileged to edit.

Thank you, too, to the Wild Goose Publications team: Susie Hay, Alex O'Neill, Jane Darroch Riley and Sandra Kramer for their professionalism and support, and to Neil Paynter, whose advice and attention to detail I value greatly.

For those of us who write liturgy, in and out of season, I offer a reflection:

> *Is thinking praying?*
>
> When I write prayers
> I think about God,
> about what I'm writing.
> I read my prayer out loud
> to hear its rhythm and sound.
> I listen to myself reading.
>
> Is what I'm creating a draft prayer?
> Do I want to type it and send it,
> or save it for some later
> polishing and editing?

Or in the thinking and writing
and reading and listening
has it already been sent?

At what stage in this process
do you hear me, God?

I can hear you chuckle at
the daftness of my question.

I can feel you smile.

Ruth Burgess, autumn (going on winter) 2016

Winter in November

A prayer for growth in winter

God our untiring Creator, who gave
hours of darkness for our rest
and times of winter for silent growth,
we give you our thanks
for the creativity of relaxation
and for the hours that refresh us.

We ask you to encourage us
through the hard times
when prospects are bleak
and the landscape is barren.

By the power of your Spirit,
bring us out of these growing places
into a space where we may flourish
with renewed understanding
of your deep desire and love,
for the sake of your Son
in whose name we pray.

Terry Garley

The Penmon robin

Five friends walked a path at Penmon,
in the week before Advent,
and a robin came to see what we were at:

cocked head, feathers fluffed out – surprising
with a blush of red – took wing, landed on
a winter twig, quizzical, sizing us up,

then flew down to our feet; a watchful, trusting
presence, always a few paces ahead,
all the way to St Seiriol's holy well.

We'd come weary and empty-handed –
we had no bread to share – but found
we walked on holy ground on that grey day

and were well-blessed: our pilgrimage
having such steadfast accompaniment:
encouragement every step of the way.

Jan Sutch Pickard

Winter haiku

dandelion clock
spores coated in sparkling frost –
tiny frozen stars

clothes over heaters
pouring of incessant rain
time to hibernate

wind-blown rose
chairs toppled on sodden grass
November garden

wind-chimes wild jangle
rain batters sun porch window
inside I cower

branches almost bare
raindrops quiveringly cling
a solitary leaf.

Mary Hanrahan

A bit of a blow

The wind on the moors
is so strong
it's blowing me over.

If God's in it
he's trying very hard
to tell me something.

The wind on the moors.
It's strong.
It's blowing me over.

Robert Shooter

The day of the storm

Through driving rain and howling wind
You call us.

When the light fades and a blanket of grey sky
reflects our moods, our fears, our darkness
You call us.

From the comfort of our homes
where we feel safe and secure, comfortable and content
You call us back into life.

Katy Owen

Remind me: a prayer during winter's storms

Life spreads out before me,
an unpredictable expanse of steely water.
The wind whips up a storm,
the waves tower high around me,
the sky is hidden by darkness.

The shore is beyond the reach of my mind.
My little boat tosses and flips in the water –
too small to be significant;
too loved to be turned away.

My Lord to whom the winds answer,
remind me that your presence calms the storm.

When the storm grows strong around me,
when the water comes lashing in,
when I am the only one left,
remind me that I am never alone,
remind me of the comfort of your fortress.

My Lord to whom the waves answer,
remind me that your presence calms the storm.

Lord, Creator of all,
show me the horizon beyond the waves,
the land where I will take my rest.
Guide me through the mist,
through the uncharted waters.
Lead me to the shore on which I will walk with you.

My Lord to whom the clouds answer,
remind me that your presence calms the storm.

When the thunder deafens me,
when the lightning blinds me,
when I am caught in the storm,
remind me who you are.
Spread your arms wide to save me.
Welcome home your lost child.

My Lord, to whom the storms answer,
stay by me,
fill me with your peace.

Kira Taylor

A blink of sun

After Laudato Si
(Tune: 'Vriede in handen', John L. Bell, 8787)

A blink of sun, a smirr of rain:
the beauty of creation –
our common home, our common weal:
no more the wealth of nations.

In thrall to profit, lost in gain,
the poor, the earth, neglected:
O touch our hearts, transform each mind:
our common home respected.

All that exists you hug in love:
compassion for all creatures.
Fill us with peace that we may live
your covenant, O teacher.

Each one, forgotten of this earth,
so precious to the Makar;
may we protect, not prey on earth,
sow beauty, not pollution.

Renew our bond with everything,
make one, a revolution:
We journey to your light unbound,
the rainbow home of nations.

A blink of sun, a smirr of rain,
on town, or field, on machair:
our common home, our common weal:
the gifts of God's creation.

da Noust

Like November

Like November, late-autumn colours my years.
Swallows, like children and grandchildren,
have flown so far away.

Foggy, gloomy days that can't be brightened
with fireworks and sparklers,
herald in Christ the King.

Advent calls: Hear my cry.
Dark December days where candles flicker
and fires warm; I sit alone.

Winter solstice passes, Northern Lights shine.
A special light: a saviour is born.
Wise men follow a star to bow before their king.

Bleak January passes: a lone majestic snowdrop
pushes its way through frosty earth.
It warms me.

When winter colours clothe and close my life
it is certain my hopes will come again
and swallows eventually return.

Sarah Pascoe

Red lantern of light

Red lantern in the morning sky,
rising through the barren trees,
scattering your light to greet another day,
fill our souls with life,
light our way.

Red lantern in the evening sky,
benediction for the day,
bring peace that passes understanding,
give rest to weary souls.

Red lantern of light,
shine rays of hope
into our nights and days.

Rebeka Maples

Souls and saints

We are part of each other

Those who have died live in their friends and families,
those who have died live in you,
those who have died live in me.

Living and dying we are part of each other,
touched by eternity,
circled in love.

Ruth Burgess

Really, God?

Really, God?
We're all in that communion of saints?
All belonging to that unbroken line?
All bound together?
Seriously?
So, my great-grandfather with his collarless shirts
and starched collars that he wore on a Sunday,
and my great-uncle Charlie with the Brylcreemed hair
who wore braces on his trousers,
and my great-aunt Nancy with the brown lace-ups
who always smelled of mothballs,
and wee auntie Annie who always wore a pinny
with a duster in the pocket and a hairnet over her curlers,
except on a Sunday,
they're all saints,
along with old Mrs Brown who sits at the back now
always with a wee sweetie to keep the wee ones quiet,
and young Kylie who takes the youth group and is the height of fashion,
and even old grumpy Bob who's always complaining,
and that wee devil Ross who winds up all the other kids;
you're telling me that they are all saints?
And even more scary,
you're telling me that I have to love them

because they're all part of your one, big, happy family?
Come on, God, give us a break.
Please!

Spill the Beans

Reflection for All Souls' Day

'I don't get the resurrection,' she said,
as she sat on the sand looking at the waves,
thinking of the one she loved who had died.
She sifted the sand through her fingers.
Ashes to ashes, dust to dust.
How much ancient death is here in these grains of sand?
'I don't get the resurrection,' she said.

'I don't get the resurrection,' she said,
as she walked through the bushland blackened by fire.
They say that some seeds only germinate after fire has raged:
life after death.
But what does that mean for us human ones?
'I don't get the resurrection,' she said.

'I don't get the resurrection,' she said,
as she sat in her winter garden staring at the bare branches of the oak tree,
remembering the one she loved who had died.
'I know, God,
you tell me that if I look close
I'll see tiny pale green leaves growing on those branches.
But what does this mean for us human ones?
I don't get the resurrection,' she said.

She put her head in her hands.

When she opened her eyes minutes later
she found herself in another garden.
It was dark and she was surrounded by olive trees.
He was beside her.
'What are you most afraid of losing?' he said.

She thought about her treasures.
There were the obvious ones like her earrings.
She liked earrings,
little stones circled in gold that dangling caught the light.
Not that.
It wasn't that she was afraid of losing.

She thought about her books.
She loved books.
Stories in which to hide and strangely find oneself.
Books about God and praying.
Not those either.

She thought about meals.
She loved preparing food for family, friends.
Remembering their favourite food and gathering them for a meal.
Not even that, she thought.
It's not even that I am most afraid of losing.

She looked at him.
'This,' she said.
'This is what I am most afraid of losing.'

'What, fear?' he said, smiling at her.
'No.
No, not that. I'll be glad to leave that behind.
You always say: don't be afraid.
Even to those poor disciples terrified in the boat in that storm,
you said: don't be afraid.
But you were afraid, in this garden, you were afraid.'
'Yes, I was,' he said.

'No, it's this, this is what I am most afraid of losing.
The company, the conversation.
With you most of all.
But with all the dear souls.
With all my dear souls.'

'Come on,' he said.
'We're going for a walk.'

'Where?' she said.
'Along that road.'
'What road?' she said.
'Have I been with you all this time and you don't know?' he said.
'Oh,' she smiled at him, 'the Emmaus road.
Are you going to open the scriptures for me too?'

They walked for a while.
'After I had died,' he said, 'when I came back, what of me remained?'
'I don't know,' she said.
'I've tried to work it out, but I don't know.
Something, something of you remained.
When you fed them bread and fish, was it real bread, real fish?'
'Does it matter?' he said.
'I don't know, but you fed them.'
'Yes,' he said.

'And Mary, when Mary saw you she didn't recognise you.
How could she not have recognised you?
I'm sure I would have recognised you,
or maybe not.
She knew you when you spoke her name,
and you wouldn't let her touch you,
as if you knew she didn't need that.
Is it that, what we can't touch, death can't take away?

'But Thomas was sure he had to touch you
and you would have let him.
But when you talked to him
he didn't need to, talking to you was enough.

'I know what remained of you when you came back after you died.
The company, the conversation.
That's what remained of you.'
'Something like that,' he said.

They walked on a little way
and then they sat down beside the Emmaus road
and she rested her head in her arms.

When she lifted her head and looked around
she saw that she was back in her own garden.
She found herself remembering again
the one she loved who had died.

'I don't get the resurrection,' she said.
But she smiled to herself,
and for just a little while,
her soul was calm.

Jenny Wilson

A liturgy of death and new life
St Winefride (Gwenfrewi), 3rd November

Place a table in the centre of the worship space, covered with a black cloth and a lit candle.

Gathering:

You call us into the darkness:
Face us with your truth.

You tell us not to worry:
Fill us with your peace.

You encourage us to face our fears:
Surround us with your love.

You call us to new paths:
Uphold us with your resurrection promise.

Song: 'Now the green blade riseth' (CH4 417) or 'When we are living, we are in the Lord' (CH4 726)

Telling the story:

St Winefride or Gwenfrewi was a seventh-century Welsh nun. Her story was recorded in the twelfth century. St Beuno, a Welsh monk, was her uncle. As a young girl Gwenfrewi felt called to be a nun, but when alone on the hills was pursued by a Welsh prince – Caradog. When Gwenfrewi refused Caradog's advances, he cut off her head with his sword. St Beuno appeared at the scene, cursed Caradog, the earth opened and swallowed Caradog and then closed up again. Beuno replaced Gwenfrewi's head on her shoulders and prayed for her and she was restored to life.

Later Gwenfrewi did become a nun, and eventually the abbess at Gwytherin until she died. Her grave at Gwytherin was regularly visited by pilgrims, until her body was taken to Shrewsbury in 1138.

A legend is told that where Gwenfrewi's head fell to the ground, a spring of healing water appeared. This place later became the shrine at Holywell in North Wales, which is still a place of pilgrimage today.

Reading: Judges 19

Extinguish the candle following this reading.

Prayer:

For too long churches have ignored or even colluded with the abuse of women. And there is a long history across cultures, throughout the world, of honour being valued above humanity.

God of all life, we pray for those who are killed or disfigured or maimed … *(leave space for names to be spoken)* …

**Challenge us when we justify,
confront us when we judge.
Enable us to stand up with courage.
Be in us with strength to intervene.**

Reading: John 8:3–11a

Prayer:

God of compassion, we pray for those who suffer *(leave space for names to be spoken)* …

**Challenge us when we ignore abuse,
confront us when we collude with violence.**

Shame us when we blame the one who is hurt.
Give power to our cries for justice and transformation.

Reading: I John 1:6–7a

Prayer:

God of justice, we pray for all people in difficult situations *(leave space for names to be spoken)* …

Challenge us when we do not recognise the humanity of each other, confront us when we value respectability over respect.
Encourage us to see you in each person.
Underwrite our solidarity. Amen

Song: 'The Lord is my light' (from *I Will Not Sing Alone*, John L. Bell, Wild Goose Publications)

Reflection:

What does 'resurrection' mean? Renewed life or new life? Was Gwenfrewi resurrected or resuscitated? … For many who have confronted death, what life that follows has a flavour of resurrection. For the individual who has faced the stark bleak truth, and gone beyond it, there is new life, a new path to travel, not a return to the old one.

In what ways have you experienced resurrection? …

Silence, during which the candle is re-lit.

Song: 'We cannot measure how you heal' (CH4 718) or 'Today I live, one day shall come my death' (CH4 725) or 'In the bulb there is a flower' (CH4 727)

Action: Building a rainbow

Using colour – cloths, candles, flowers – be creative – transform the space from bleakness to vibrancy.

Music during the action: 'Don't be afraid', John L. Bell, from Come All You People, *Wild Goose Publications*, or 'Behold, I make all things new', John L. Bell, *from* Come All You People

In building this rainbow we are blessing:
those who have been abused,
those who support them
and those who are making a stand against violence and injustice.

We choose to embrace liberation, respect and integrity.
We choose to grow, to thrive, to blossom in new life.
We choose to take the risk of trusting – ourselves, each other and God.
We commit to God's path and promise of new life.

Affirmation:

We believe in a God who sees potential,
who brings colour into our world
and delights in all creation.

We believe in a God who hurts when we hurt,
who holds us and confronts us
and stands beside us in solidarity.

We believe in a God who is with us in each breath,
who amazes us and shocks us
and invites us to join the dance.

We believe that life is God's gift. Hallelujah!

Song: 'Christ is alive' (CH4 422) or 'Haven't you heard that Jesus is risen?' (CH4 433) or 'One more step' (CH4 530)

Blessing:

May God who cares for us,
who stands with us,
who inspires us,
bless us as we journey
into the unknown.

May we be beacons of your light and truth
and wellsprings of your love and hope.
Amen

Zam Walker

In steps of saints

Words: Carol Dixon. Music: Greta Wrigley.

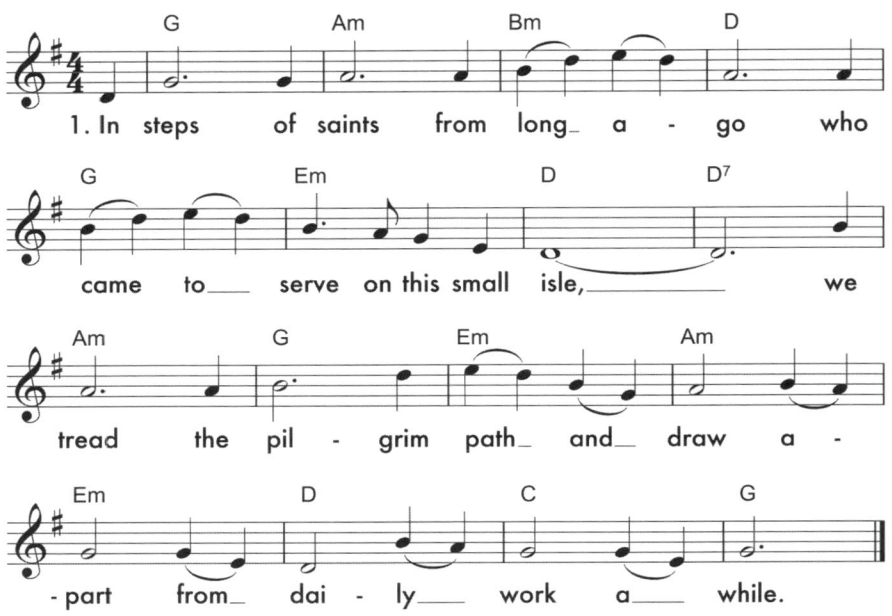

Words © Carol Dixon, Music © Greta Wrigley

In steps of saints from long ago
who came to serve on this small isle,
we tread the pilgrim path and draw
apart from daily work a while.

We share our journey on the way
with others searching too for peace,
and find God present in each one
who honestly and humbly seeks.

We long for space to hear God's voice
and find it in the milling crowd,
as well as hushed in holy church
at prayer, in silence and aloud.

We gaze upon the sunlit sea
or stroll along in mist and rain,
rejoicing that our God is seen
and understood in joy and pain.

In steps of saints we travel on
forever changed, yet still the same;
we serve and follow in Christ's way
in daily work, to praise his name.

Words: Carol Dixon, music: Greta Wrigley

We give thanks

Generous God
we thank you for the pointers and signs
that remind us of your love,
your constancy
and call to action.

We give thanks
for those wise, wonderful,
and often ordinary, people
who have altered the paths of our lives.

Fiona Barker

Prayers for an All Saints' Communion

The invitation

Come all who give thanks for the gift of life.
Come all who long for a just and happy world.
Come all who seek peace and pursue it;
and together we will work
transforming
pain into hope,
fear into love,
crying into laughter.

**We join hands
with the living
who are learning to love;**

**we dance
with the dead
whose vision still lives;**

**we pause
with the angels
in remembrance.**

Post-communion prayer

Lover, beholder of my being
Lover, reaching out to me
Lover, beckoning me to love
You feed me

Jesus, calmer of the distressed
Jesus, lifter of those who fall
Jesus, carrier of the weak
You feed me

Spirit, quencher of my thirst
Spirit, companion in my loneliness

Spirit, guardian of my soul
You feed me

In solidarity with the saints
we have shared this meal

In confidence with the faithful
we have gathered our prayers

In faithfulness with those you love
**you have made your presence known
and we have been fed.**

Saints blessing

We join hands of blessing
with saints and angels

**beautiful and plain
wise and foolish
weak and strong**

We receive a blessing
from each other

**forgiving and forgiven
understanding and understood
healing and healed**

This is God's blessing
to us and through us

**for the earth …
and for all longing to be loved.**

Elizabeth Baxter

St Lucy's Day (December 13th)

You come to my door dressed in white, early in the morning. You came last year, too, which makes it a tradition. At your age, a second time does that. *We always, we always*, you say, and your mother catches my eye. We smile.

Your brothers come up behind you with paper lanterns strung on sticks, like luminous fish caught in December's not-quite dawn. They jostle on the step, and I open the door wide to let them in, the morning air outside crisp, clouding our breath, the frost white on the hedge.

Across the street, the milk lorry has pulled up on the pavement, and the man unloads his delivery for the shop. The café around the corner is not yet open. At the end of the street, trees point their bony fingers to the sky.

You linger and smile shyly on the doorstep, the candles on your crown ablaze. They are just electric candles, made of white plastic, and the crown itself is green felt, but you look lovely. You are so excited, standing there with a basket of treats to share, but you are also careful to stand up straight and tall so your crown stays balanced.

This is a new story for me. Lucy and the light. Before I moved here, each December started slowly, bringing memories of my grandmother. Her birthday comes early in the month, and so does the anniversary of her death. Strange how dates can coincide like that. She had forgotten so much by the time she died, so many years collapsed and swept away in confusion. My mum wondered if she might have held on for December, somehow waiting, but not knowing what she waited for.

She would have liked to see you as you are now. She was always kind to small people. You hold out your basket, and I pull back the tea towel to see saffron buns, each twisted like a double snail, the centres marked with currants. There were snails in my granny's garden. I remember that. The broken shells and the thrush's anvil like something out of a fairy tale.

Last year, you told me St Lucy's story – how she visited Christians in the catacombs, wearing a wreath of candles on her head to leave her hands free so that she might carry as much food as possible. Another fairy-tale image, these stories we carry in our hearts.

On the radio this morning, there was a threat of high winds. They might close the bridge, even send the kids home early from school. You'd like that. An afternoon suddenly open for books on the sofa or in your private place behind the curtain. I see you there sometimes when I walk past your house, but don't worry, I won't tell.

Or maybe you will spend the time at the table with your paintbox. This is the season for making cards, of course, and I know you love purple, deep-sky purple, then gold bright like stars. Pop one through my letterbox, will you? I would like to hold it in my hands and look into that light.

Katie Munnik

A prayer for All Saints'

As we remember loved ones who have died,
be near to us, ever-living God,
and bring to us your comfort.
You know our grief
and understand all we feel.
Walk with us as we learn to live with loss;
help us to comfort and support one another.
May your compassion surround us,
may your strength sustain us,
that in the days to come
we may see not only our sorrow
but the dawning of hope
in the Christ who died
yet lives again.
Amen

Simon Taylor

What I miss when I am missing you

In memory of Cesar Espiritu

What I miss when I am missing you:
the splendour of your otherness and its irritation:
the frustration that I could not understand you easily,
no self-evident jokes, no shared extravaganza.
There remained a distance
that moment of translation
but your hands were gentle and their language delicate.

I miss the way you said things indirectly;
of course, it also made me mad.
Why couldn't you call a spade a spade?
Why couldn't you just speak what I called the truth?
With you it became so elusive,
lost itself in your concern that none of your words
should cause people to lose face.

Still, I miss the one hundred hidden ways you could say
I love you.

I miss your clarity when it came to denouncing the dictator and his cronies
and the sickly rich in their fantastic palaces.
I understand now why sometimes
you were afraid for your life,
as I watch the shameless violence that shields the eternal idol
mammon.

I miss the discoveries I made because of you;
there was a different world out there
waiting to be recognised and respected.

I miss the moments when we beheld
the image of God in each other,
vulnerable and splendid beyond words.

I miss the beauty of it.

Reinhild Traitler-Espiritu

Saints alive

At the start of his first letter to the Corinthians Paul puts the call to be saints into true perspective:

'Consider your own calling, brothers and sisters; not many of you were wise by human standards; not many were powerful, not many were of noble birth. But God chose what is foolish in the world's eyes to shame the wise; God chose what is weak in the world's eyes to shame the strong. God chose what is low and despised.'

We need a shift of focus to do justice to Paul's observation on who are saints of God.

Take the woman abandoned by her husband who takes on ill-paid bits of jobs, exhausting herself to feed and clothe her children. She may have to work in church time and think she is no great shakes as a Christian. Take the man with a history of drink and drugs who goes successfully into rehab: who fights the temptation, again and again, to give in to bodily cravings, and overcomes at cost the temptation to give in. Attested miracles are called for? Neighbours all around will affirm these miracles.

Take the village where I live, where, without any fuss or publicity, that child is cared for, the lonely one visited, the one who thinks of himself/herself as useless is invited to lend a hand; where cheerful, social events call on the gifts of many. My second eye joins the first in a haemorrhage. There is a knock on my back door. It is my neighbour across the way who calls himself a secularist: 'I've heard about the damage which stops you reading and writing. When you need to go to hospital, I'll take you, and I'll wait as long as need be to take you back. If you need someone to read to you, I'm available.' Just that. An offer, detailed and put on the table. No fuss, just natural kindness.

A programme on TV detailed the disaster, sometimes heart-rending, suffered in the recent floods. But it could not end there. It dealt with emergency organisations taking people to safety from inundated homes, with neighbours taking up mops to help clear up. Halls were made into reception centres with beds for the night and hot meals provided.

The saints of God are not on calendars.

They are all around our doors.

Ian M Fraser

They're all around us

St Lucy stopped for a moment,
while she rested her arms and legs,
from pushing her little
brother down the sidewalk
in his electric car whose
battery had run down;
stroking Maya's nose,
her eyes shimmered with delight
and she exploded in a giggle,
'You're a silly dog!'
when she suddenly baptised her
with a sloppy kiss.

Pausing for a few moments
from helping his elderly neighbour,
St Chuck leaned on his rake,
smiling as his grandkids
eagerly and deliberately
scattered the leaves he had
spent all afternoon
piling by the curb,
whispering, 'What a life!'

Slowly, painstakingly, as if
she were joining together a puzzle,
differently-abled St Jennifer
put each item in its place
in the cloth bags,

not making them too heavy
(as the customer requested),
making sure the bread
ended up on top,
and nothing too heavy
was near the eggs.

They're all around us, aren't they,
those precious drops of grace
sprinkled in our lives?

Thom M Shuman

Remembrance

From the darkness of death

From the darkness of death,
God calls us into glorious light.

From the tumult of war,
God call us into the beauty of peace.

Children of light,
God calls us today to remembrance.

In light and in peace,
We will remember them.

Ask for representatives from each generation (a child, a teenager, someone in their 20s, 30s ...) and if you have uniformed organisations present, ask for a representative from each of those groups. Ask each person to come and place a poppy (a sign of remembering) on a low table and to light a candle, as a sign of our willingness to live as children of light.

A time of silence follows.

Through our living may your light shine
and through our prayers may your love be known.
Amen

Spill the Beans

They shall not grow old

Congregation stands.

An older person says:

'They shall not grow old,
as we that are left grow old.
Age shall not weary them,
nor the years condemn.'

A younger person says:

'At the going down of the sun
and in the morning,
we will remember them.' (Laurence Binyon)

We will remember them.

Silence follows (2 minutes).

The completion of the silence can be indicated by the playing of a suitable piece of music or when the worship leader continues in prayer.

Ever-living God,
today we remember those
whom you have gathered
from the noise and storm of war
into the peace of your presence.

May that same Spirit of peace
fall on us and all who remember this day,
particularly those whose remembering
brings back memories
of personal loss and tragedy.

Grant us your peace,
bring justice to all peoples
and establish harmony
amongst all nations and races,
through Jesus Christ we pray. Amen

Keith Blackwood, Spill the Beans

We commend to you

Almighty God,
in your heart we find mercy and peace.

This day we commend to you the men and women who serve
in the Navy, Army and Air Force,
who face danger, and who put their own safety at risk
in order to secure peace for others.
Help them to know that, although often far from home,
out of reach of the touch of a lover,
out of reach of the playful cuddle of a child,
they are never beyond the reach of your touch and care.
We pray that in all the actions of those who serve in war,
or in peacekeeping activities around the world,
the vision of your love for all people is neither lost nor forgotten.

We pray this day for the families of those who serve overseas.
In their loneliness and anxiety
may your Spirit bring support and comfort
in order that they find the strength to endure their time apart
from loved ones.

We pray especially
on this Remembrance Sunday
for those who have lost their lives in war,
and their families who need support in their time of grief.
We pray, too, for those maimed in battle
and we pray for the medical professionals whose skills, care and attention
are used in rehabilitation.

We pray in Jesus' name. Amen

Keith Blackwood, Spill the Beans

A response for Remembrance Day

We fight over land that is not ours.
Forgive us our arrogance.

We put a price on resources that are priceless.
Forgive us our greed.

We create divisions and labels that separate and humiliate.
Forgive us our hurtfulness.

Too often we fail to learn from our mistakes and reconcile our errors.
Forgive us our wrongdoings.
We will remember that the earth is the Lord's and all that is in it.

Fiona van Wissen

Loving God

Loving God,
when war comes
be with us and our enemies.

Be with those who fight,
those who get hurt,
those who die,
those whose lives are changed forever.

Loving God,
be with us in our pain,
our questions,
our sadness and despair.

Hallow our lives
with your peace,
your justice
and your forgiving love.

Ruth Burgess

The ordinary people

We remember today all the ordinary people
ripped from their towns and villages,
torn from their families
to serve their country in war.

We remember today the people
left behind to keep things going
in factories, on farms, on the streets blitzed by war.

We remember today the people
who lost their lives in war
and those left behind who never saw their loved ones again,
who grew up without a parent, a sibling, a partner or a friend,
who never discovered love again
and who grew old alone.

We remember today all the ordinary people
on either side of the conflict whose lives were changed forever,
all those who paid the price of freedom.

And, in our remembering the ordinary people,
we remember that the cost of war will always be too high
and paid for by ordinary people.

Liz Crumlish, Spill the Beans

Seeking the ways of peace

Deep, searching God,
who has taught us
to love our enemies,
and do good to those who hate us,
give us, we pray, the courage
which delivers us from the dread of our foes.

Show us that your love can overcome fear
and take away our demonising
of those who are different from us.

Restore us to the harmony you intended
for the whole human race.

Guide people of all faiths and no faith
into your ways of peace and justice.

This we ask in and through your Spirit
of freedom, truth and mercy.

Terry Garley

Let us go from this place

Let us go from this place
with minds that never forget,
with hearts that grow in hope,
with lives that shine Christ's light.

Let us go to serve,
to reconcile,
to bring peace
and to stand united
as children of the light.

And may the blessing of God,
Creator, Peacemaker, Peace-bringer,
go with us all
this day and every day. Amen

Roddy Hamilton, Spill the Beans

Thanksgiving Thursday and Black Friday

Another leaf in the table

Let us give
thanks
in this season,
by putting another
leaf in the table: to
make room for those
who are always
serving us (even
while we quibble over
their gratuity);

let us find the
Baby
this year,
by affirming
the giftedness
of those
whose lives
we too often
ignore.

Thom M Shuman

Thanksgiving

Food features a lot
in the life
and stories
of Jesus.

At mealtimes
a lot of discussion,
both comfortable
and challenging,
takes place.

Surprising people
take their
places
as guests
and hosts
around the
table with
Jesus.

No one
is ever sure
quite who and
what to expect!

It's thanksgiving.

Come and share food
and laughter
and tears
and stories.

Come and give thanks.

Welcome to the feast.

Ruth Burgess

Thank you

Thank you
for food to share
for family
for friends
for smiles and stories.

Thank you
for sunshine and snow
for stars
for moonlight
for frost on windows.

Thank you
for good books
and music
for posters and paintings
and sculpture on the streets.

Thank you
for computers –
they're amazing!

Thank you
for making me, me.
Thank you for being you.
Thanks for hope
and tears
and laughter.

Generous giver,
breath of life,
God of love
and surprises,
thank you.

Ruth Burgess

The mall is my shepherd

The mall is my shepherd,
I shall always need more.

It makes me lie down in mattress stores;
it leads me beside coffee shops;
it restores my greed.
It leads me down paths for the sake of its sales.

Even though I walk the aisles of outlet stores,
I am not afraid,
for you are at my side:
your credit cards and coupons – they comfort me.

You prepare a feast for me at the food court
in the midst of shoving shoppers;
you anoint me with cappuccinos,
my latte overflows.

Surely stress and debt shall follow me
all the days of my life (and of my kids' lives),
and I shall live at the mall
every day of my life.

Thom M Shuman

Prayer for Black Friday

Lord, teach us to live simply.
Free us from the urge to drive a bargain over our neighbour;
for a bargain for me on Black Friday
may mean higher prices for others the rest of the year.
Free us all from our fear of missing out,
and may your kingdom come through our simplicity.
Amen

da Noust

Buy Nothing Day

'Buy Nothing Day'
competing with 'Black Friday',
when cheap bargains are available
at the end of November.
Of course if you really need that bargain
it might be fair enough.
But a hyped up spending spree that has attached itself to Christmas.
Nobody needs that.

People dressed as zombies wandering around shopping malls;
lines of people pushing trolleys round supermarkets.
We don't need all that stuff.
We can certainly manage without it for one day,
and we might even find we can manage with less every day.

We used to have a day of buying nothing every week.
Called Sunday, the Christian Sabbath,
or Saturday, the Jewish Sabbath.
For many these days still mean something,
but for many they have an image problem.
Too often they are associated with long faces and strict rules
rather than the day of rest they were supposed to be.

Let's celebrate the fun that 'Buy Nothing Day' can be,
the anti-materialism that could appeal to people of all religions and none;
let's share the chance to reflect on spending habits,
on where and who we buy from,
whether we use cash or card, money we have, or don't have.
Who produces, transports, markets the things we usually buy …

It's not about never buying;
it's one day of saying stop: think.
Banish 'Black Friday',
bless 'Buy Nothing Day':
you don't have to do anything, you can just do nothing,
or at least buy nothing, all day …

Liz Gibson

Black Friday!

I refuse to buy
the paranoia
that is marked
down today,
in hopes that
it might become
a holy day
for those who
need blessings the most.

Thom M Shuman

Christ the King/ The reign of God

You I could follow

King of kings
Lord of lords
Glory hallelujah!
Really?
Are these words just
a neat, peppy praise song,
fun to sing
but empty of meaning?

No kings around here
that I know of,
but a lot of politicians
who act as if folk
are agin' 'em
if you are not with them;

no lords around here,
except those who
think they can
lord it over everyone else,
while debt and worry and fear
control my life;

glory seems to be
in short supply these
days,
and hallelujahs
don't seem to mean much
to most folk;

but you

you are a mystery solved
in the impossibilities
of life;
an enigma wrapped
in wonder;
a majesty born

in humility;
a life blossoming
out of death.

And you

you I could follow
forever.

Thom M Shuman

From seed to shoot

From seed to shoot
God's kingdom is coming.
God's kingdom is coming near.

From shoot to branch
God's kingdom is coming.
God's kingdom is coming near.

Rooted and growing
God's kingdom is coming.
God's kingdom is coming near.

Flourishing, blossoming
God's kingdom is coming.
God's kingdom is coming near.

With wisdom and might
God's kingdom is coming.
God's kingdom is coming near.

With justice and mercy
God's kingdom is coming.
God's kingdom is coming near.

With righteousness and faithfulness
God's kingdom is coming.
God's kingdom is coming near.

Nikki Macdonald, Spill the Beans

The Christian year

Andy: Well, that's it all over, Ada.

Ada: What's all over, Andy?

Andy: The Christian Year.

Ada: I thought every year was a Christian year.

Andy: Well, to us it is, but the liturgical year.

Ada: The what-ical year?

Andy: Liturgical year! You know, it starts with Advent, then we have Christmas and Epiphany, then Lent, Easter, Pentecost, then there is some Ordinary time, and back to Advent again, with a couple of festivals like Harvest, All Saints', Remembrance Day and Guild Sunday in between.

Ada: You know, Andy, you never cease to amaze me with your knowledge of the church!

Andy: Oh – I thought everybody knew that!

Ada: Why not ask the congregation how much they know about the different Christian seasons?

Andy: Aye, that would be good fun, testing their knowledge of what those different seasons mean.

Ada: Oh, Andy, look at their faces. Big Jim is hiding behind the pew. Wee Mary over there has turned pure white!

Andy: Aye, and Isobel over there, she is looking a bit sheepish after coming last in the church quiz. And the minister – oh, he has just disappeared!

Ada: Aye, they don't all look so smart now.

Andy: Shall I start with the first question, Ada?

Ada: You go for it, Andy!

Andy: Ach, maybe better not to make them suffer and feel small.

Christ the King/The reign of God

Ada: You are a man of real compassion, Andy, not wanting to put them to shame. But why do we have a liturgical year anyway?

Andy: Well, Ada, remember the passage we heard from Revelation this morning where it said that God was the Alpha and the Omega?

Ada: Is that the cars God owns?

Andy: Eh – what?

Ada: Does it mean that God has an Alfa Romeo and a Vauxhall Omega for getting around the world quickly?

Andy: Ada, I am seriously worried about you. Alpha and Omega are the first and last letters of the Greek alphabet, and it means that God is the beginning and the end.

Ada: The beginning and the end?

Andy: Yes, God was at the beginning of the world and will be at the end. The Liturgical Year helps us to explore the main themes of our faith, like how God came into the world, how he died and rose again, and how he gave us the gift of the Holy Spirit.

Ada: So Advent, Christmas and Epiphany tell us the story of the beginning and God coming into the world.

Andy: Lent and Easter tells us about Jesus' ministry and of his death and resurrection.

Ada: Pentecost celebrates the coming of the Holy Spirit.

Andy: And Ordinary time explores other major themes in the Bible, like the miracles, and some of the great prophets and stories from the Old Testament.

Ada: So everything we need to know about God can be found in the Bible, and we cover it in one year?

Andy: Well, actually it takes nearly three years to cover the whole of the Bible and all its major themes, and each year is divided into cycles, A, B and C.

Ada: So we start at the beginning and go to the end of the Bible.

Andy: Not quite, it jumps about a little, but over the three years we get a big picture of God, and then we begin the cycle all over again.

Ada: So this last Sunday in the liturgical year is a bit like Hogmanay: we look back at the old and forward to the new.

Andy: That's nicely put, Ada.

Ada: Thanks, Andy – and a happy New Year to you when it comes!

John Murning, Spill the Beans

Christ reigns

Four people behind the communion table, each in turn leading one of these actions:

We take purple: *rip a purple sheet and lay it on the communion table.*

We lay a crown of thorns: *lift a crown of thorns and lay it on the communion table.*

We break bread: *break crusty bread so there are lots of crumbs and lay it on the communion table.*

We place a cross: *place a cross on the communion table.*

These are the symbols of our Lord, Jesus Christ,
rich in the life he gave for others,
rich in the grace he offers all.

This is Reign of Christ Sunday, the last Sunday of the church year.
These are the symbols of our Lord Jesus.
Let us worship.

Christ, reigning.
When the first are last,
you reign.
When hearers hear,
you reign.

When the heavy-laden find rest,
you reign.

This is a peculiar reign:
a glory that can only reflect
from tarnished gold,
an audience given only to broken angels,
a banquet set out for the least of these.

This is a peculiar reign:
the world shifts on its axis,
the darkness creeps back,
the forgotten find themselves with names.

This is the reign we long for,
the realm we dream of,
the community we believe in.

May we live dangerously
and turn our words of faith into acts of trust.
May we be part of this, O Christ:
May we lift your torn robe and wrap the poor in it.
May we take your crown of thorns and stand with the suffering.
May we break the bread and feed the hungry of the world.
May we hold the cross and know what must be given.

This is a peculiar reign,
but it is yours
and it will change the world,
if only we would find you,
follow you
and worship you
in this way.

Christ,
reigning.
Make space for us
and may we make space for you.
So be it. Amen

Roddy Hamilton, Spill the Beans

Opening responses

Make way!
Make space!

Make time!
Make peace!

The Lord our King is close.
The King of Love is near.

The Prince of Peace approaches.
Make way for Christ the King.

Peter Johnston, Spill the Beans

Closing prayer

Christ is King.
Christ reigns,
but there in the background
(can you hear it?),
the whisper of the prophets.

Christ is King.
Soon to be born among us,
but let us go now
as the year turns.

Christ reigns
in the hopes of the people.

Roddy Hamilton, Spill the Beans

The king and the castle

(Script to be read by two children, loosely based around Isaiah 11:1–5)

Project work for Mr Mackenzie:

Read the profile of the king and design a castle for him to live and work in.

A castle – that should be good.

OK – here's the profile of the king:

The king is wise and strong and he listens to people.
The king wants to do what pleases God.
The king doesn't judge people by their appearance or listen to gossip about them.
The king defends the helpless and gives poor people justice.
The king punishes the wicked.
Each morning the king pulls on work clothes and strong boots and builds justice and hope in his lands.

He sounds a good guy – let's design him a great castle.

Big stone castle I think – impressive.

With a huge moat.

Why a moat, does he need that?

He needs to keep out his enemies – make it hard for them to get in.

Got that, but it says the king listens to people, poor people, helpless people, so they need to be able to come to the castle and talk to him, so we can't make it too hard to get in.

OK – scrap the moat.

We could keep it and stock it with fish and lend out fishing rods to the people who come to see the king – they could take any fish they caught home for their supper!

They could – now, how about dungeons?

Dungeons?

Yeah – big damp spooky ones, with chains on the walls, and rats.

Rats?

Well, it says the king punishes the wicked.

Mmm – but does he punish them by putting them in dungeons and forgetting all about them? – he's a wise and a just king remember – he might want to talk to them and find ways to help them.

He might – but let's keep the dungeons anyway – I really fancy designing those.

OK – what about kitchens?

Huge ones – ovens to bake bread and cakes and pies – one of those things that turns and that you can cook a whole cow on.

A spit you mean.

Yes – funny name – a spit – and he'll need someone to cook for him.

Servants I guess – we'll need rooms for them.

We can build some small rooms next to the dungeons, out of the way, be a bit damp, but they're only for the servants.

The king gives poor people justice remember – damp cramped places to live in aren't justice.

OK, we'll give them decent rooms on the middle floors.

And he'll need a throne room.

And a huge gold throne.

And a dining room.

With an enormous table.

And gold cutlery and a chandelier.

A 'chanda' what?

A chandelier – a huge light with dangly bits of glass.

And he'll need a bedroom.

With a four-poster bed.

And a huge wardrobe.

A huge wardrobe?

Well, it says in the morning he pulls on work clothes and boots – he'll need somewhere to keep his clothes and his crown.

Probably better to keep his boots in the kitchen – we'll design him a special boot cupboard.

With his initials on it.

In gold leaf.

This is a great project for Mr Mackenzie – I'm really enjoying this.

Me too, but better stop now – it's time for tea.

Ruth Burgess, Spill the Beans

Waiting for a God of

(A purple robe/cloth is brought forward and placed centrally.)

King of kings,
we seek you in the leadership of our world:
in the places where power is not used with justice,
that your way will challenge those who are responsible for others;
in the people denied their human rights,
that they will make known your call for justice;
and in the times of weakness,
that we may rely on your strength and power.

For those waiting for a God of power, we pray …

(Pause)

(A lit candle is brought forward and placed centrally.)

Light of life,
we seek you in the shadows of our world:
in the places where violence and hatred thrive,
that your gift of peace will bring transformation;
in the people struggling with the darkness of depression and suffering,
that your healing will re-create wholeness;
and in the times of sadness and death,
that your Spirit of comfort will be present.

For those waiting for a God of light, we pray …

(Pause)

(An empty bowl is brought forward and placed centrally.)

Saviour of the poor,
we seek you in the needs of our world:
in the places where there is hunger and thirst,
that we might share our food and drink;
in the people who have lost hope,
that we will bear witness to your compassion;
and in the times of destruction and devastation,
that we will strive to plant and build your kingdom.

Christ the King/The reign of God

For those waiting for a God of salvation, we pray ...

(Pause)

(An open Bible is brought forward and placed centrally.)

Word of truth,
we seek you in the disbelief of our world:
in the places of deceit and mistrust,
that your honesty will always be our guide;
in the people caught up in lies and suspicion,
that your truth will set them free;
and in the times of confusion, worry and questioning,
that we will put our trust in your wisdom.

For those waiting for a God of truth, we pray ...

(Pause)

(Wooden/pottery hands are brought forward and placed centrally.)

Flesh of our flesh,
we seek you in the humanity of our world:
in the places where dignity and worth are ignored,
that the weak and vulnerable may reveal your power;
in the people we find difficult to get on with,
that our eyes will be open to recognise your presence;
and in the times of disbelief in ourselves,
that we may be given confidence by knowing we are made in your image
and likeness.

For those waiting for a God of life, we pray ...

(Pause)

King of kings
Light of life
Saviour of the poor
Word of truth
Flesh of our flesh
in your love we pray.
Amen

Peter Siney

A sending

In the strength of God the maker
we are going on a journey.

In the friendship of Jesus
we are going on a journey.

In the safeguarding of the Holy Spirit
we are going on a journey.

A star is shining.
Angels are busy.
Mary is pregnant.
Joseph is packing.
Advent is coming.
It's time to go.

May God bless us with hope and wonder as we travel.
Amen

Ruth Burgess

Advent

Poem for Advent

We must prepare a way.
Try to straighten paths made crooked
by our selfishness and compulsions.

We have forgotten the grace-filled room,
the angel's message, 'Do not fear.'
We fear the very joy he promised.

We are afraid of the journey,
the hard road, the bitter cold
and the doors slammed in our faces.

We are terrified of giving birth.

Yet within us there is such a thirst for innocence.

We must enter our hearts' dark stable,
clear away the dirty straw of resentment and pride,
soil our hands and make some effort
to find a fresher, sweeter hay of welcome,
light a candle of hope,
as we humbly await the birth of Wonder.

Mary Hanrahan

St Nicholas Day (December 6th)

A wooden shoe
waiting for a gift,
like a manger
ready to receive a blessing
from a saint on horseback.

Fiona van Wissen

Just when

Just when
we expect you to
arrive
with anger steaming out
of your ears,
you come
to sit next to us,
listening to our deepest
brokenness;

just when
we figure you will show up
to toss us in
the nearest
fire,
you come
to sweep up
the ashes
of every broken
hope,
refining them
into the chalice
of wonder;

just when
we are certain you are hiding
there
in the shadows,
ready to leap out
and scare us into
repentance,
you come
to swaddle us
in garlands of grace,
twinkling off and on
in pure joy.

Thom M Shuman

Advent wreath ceremony

Advent 1: 2 Kings 22:1–10, 23:1–3: Listen

In the beginning was the Word –
spoken and breathed,
a promise made and kept.
Listen and hear –
God's promise is true!
The Word was in the beginning,
and through him all things come into being.
Eternal and near at hand,
already and not yet,
God's promise is the foundation of all life.
Listen!
Hear the covenant anew, giving voice to a future with hope.

Candle is lit.

Advent 2: Isaiah 40:1–11: Speak

In the beginning was the Word –
spoken and breathed,
a promise made and kept.
Speak it loud and clear –
God's promise is true!
The Word was in the beginning,
and through him all things come into being.
Eternal and near at hand,
already and not yet,
God's promise is the foundation of all life.
Do not hold back!
Speak out, giving voice to God's peace that passes all understanding.

Candle is lit

Advent 3: Ezra 1:1–4, 3:1–4, 10–13: Persevere

In the beginning was the Word –
spoken and breathed,
a promise made and kept.
Persevere in hope, keep the faith –
God's promise is true!
The Word was in the beginning,
and through him all things come into being.
Eternal and near at hand,
already and not yet,
God's promise is the foundation of all life.
Keep going!
Persevere in joy, giving voice to God's presence yet again.

Candle is lit.

Advent 4: Luke 1:5–24a, 57–80: Trust

In the beginning was the Word –
spoken and breathed,
a promise made and kept.
Trust the good news –
God's promise is true!
The Word was in the beginning,
and through him all things come into being.
Eternal and near at hand,
already and not yet,
God's promise is the foundation of all life.
Trust in God!
Wait with faith, giving voice to Christ's love for all.

Candle is lit.

Christmas Eve: Glorify

In the beginning was the Word –
spoken and breathed,
a promise made and kept.
Glorify the Lord with me –
God's promise is true!

The Word was in the beginning,
and through him all things come into being.
Eternal and near at hand,
already and not yet,
God's promise is the foundation of all life.
Glory to God!
The Word is made flesh, giving voice to God's promise yet again.

Candle is lit.

Teri Carol Peterson

Gladness

Paved with credit cards,
the roads to the malls
stretch out before us
all shiny and bright,
the lights twinkling
in reds, greens and gold,
all the specials
waiting for us inside;

clambering up ladders,
prancing across the roofs –
electricity stringing
this way and that,
power-stripping
Santa, the reindeer,
as well as the itsy-bitsy
crèche –
the neighbours make ready
their houses to welcome
all the traffic to this
wonderful time of
year;

shaking your head,
you turn and look down
the shadowed alley lying
before you,
potholed by poverty,
lined with hedgerows
where peace and hope
are twisted together and
shrivelling from indifference,
gang tags sprayed on
garage doors which house
empty dreams;
you hold out your hand to us
invitingly,
'This is a shortcut I know
to Bethlehem.
You coming?'

Thom M Shuman

God approaches

Climate-change Advent,
dreich rather than cold,
wind in the trees and round the houses,
ditches full of murky water,
rare glimpses of a silvery sun.

And still God approaches,
wherever we are,
however we're feeling,
whatever the season,
bringing warmth
and hope and promises,
and surprises yet to come.

Ruth Burgess

For such mornings as this

Written in response to the tragedy at Sandy Hook Elementary in December 2012

Lord, you have been our dwelling place in all generations.
Before the mountains were brought forth,
or ever you had formed the earth and the world,
from everlasting to everlasting you are God. (Psalm 90:1–2)

Once again, we are reminded about the meaning of this bleak midwinter we call Advent. For God did not come to create a greeting card industry, nor so we could string lights on houses and trees. God did not become one of us so we might have office parties and give people things they don't really need. God was not born so songs could be written and sermons preached.

God came for such mornings as this, after the long night of anguished tossing and turning, with visions of horror dancing in our heads. God came to walk with us as we wander the streets of our hearts asking, 'How? Why? When?'

God came to huddle with terrified children in closets where school supplies are stored, and to give teachers the strength not to show their worst fears. God came to cradle the wounded and the dying, so they would know they were not abandoned in that loneliest of moments.

God came to give the first responders the courage to walk into the unspeakable, to be willing to put themselves between danger and little children. God came to gather the parents and grandparents up into the divine lap of comfort and hope, even as their arms would no longer be able to embrace their child. God came to have that most compassionate heart broken as many times as ours are, to weep with us even when we have run out of tears, to stand next to us with the same look of horror and disbelief.

God came for mornings such as this, with the same haggard face, with the same questions, with the same anger, with the same sense of loss and hopelessness, but with deep wells of grace from which we can drink, with compassion which will never end, with comforting arms which will not grow weary, with hope which stretches from everlasting to everlasting.

God came, and is still with us.

Thom M Shuman

Intercessions for Advent

Come, Lord Jesus,
into the darkness of our world;
a world where there is injustice, racial tension and war,
where many people still lack the basics of food and clean water.

Come, Lord Jesus,
into the uncertain future of migrants
who risk everything to escape atrocities
yet know that they could still end up paying with their lives.

Come, Lord Jesus,
into our communities
where many are struggling with redundancy and debt
and food banks have become a lifeline for those in need.

Come, Lord Jesus,
into the darkness of our cities
where greed and discrimination
make misery in people's lives.

Come, Lord Jesus,
into our lives
and into the lives of those for whom we are concerned.

Bring comfort to the bereaved
and to those who are struggling to cope with life on their own.

Come, Lord Jesus,
give reassurance where there is fear,
and confidence where there is doubt.
Wherever people are hurting,
come and let your light shine.
Amen

Kathy Crawford

Prayer of approach and adoration

Loving God,
we gather in this season of promise
to worship you and sing your praise.
We praise you for your love
and for your faithfulness,
for you are the source of all hope
and from you all joy springs.
You are the one we expect,
but your coming is always unexpected.
You are the one who turns everything upside down
and you make all things new.
Advent God of surprises,
we worship you
and we wait for you to awaken our wonder
and astound us with your arrival.

Loving God,
in this season of excitement and weariness
open our hearts to your presence,
for we know you meet us and hold us:
in and beyond the busyness
in and beyond the glitter
in and beyond the rush.
When we are tired and frayed,
when we lose sight of what it's all about,
when we put ourselves first
and forget that you come to bring love,
come close and restore us
and forgive us, we pray.

Loving God,
mend our broken hearts
and help us to know
ourselves forgiven and loved.

In our thankfulness
help us to wait
and to watch for you,
faithfully and truly all our days.
Amen

Louise Gough

Gaudete Sunday

Even with

no visible evidence
of hope,
except for a young woman
giving birth in the
shadows of poverty;
no resounding words
of grace,
except for the teenager
helping a Syrian child
learn a new language;
no superhero
coming to our rescue,
except for the volunteers
who ignore borders
to bring healing and kindness,

again and again,
God says,
'Rejoice!'

Thom M Shuman

A song for Gaudete Sunday

(Tune: 'Gaudete')

Chorus: Sing and dance and rejoice,
for Christ is with us,
born of Mary –
sing and dance and rejoice.

Born into a stable yard,
human, weak and lowly;
God who set the sun ablaze
makes a stable holy:

Chorus

Holy is the stable yard,
this and every other.
Holy every father's care,
every loving mother:

Chorus

God is with his people now,
in his world beside them,
bursting wide the prophet's gates:
nothing can divide them:

Chorus

Roddy Cowie

God in the dark

Holy God,
before us, beside us, within us,
there is no place without you;
help us to recognise your presence
in the dark places,
the difficult places, of our lives;
even as we sing of your glory
in the light.
Amen

Chris Polhill

Advent call

Come, Christ, come:
Come with your word.

Come, Sophia, come:
Come with your wisdom.

Come, Christa, come:
Come with your embrace.

Come, Jesus, come:
Come with your playfulness.

Come, Mary, come:
Inspire us with your Yes.

Elizabeth Baxter

Responses and prayers for the Sunday before Christmas

Opening responses

This is Magnificat:
The powerful unseated

The proud scattered
The little people lifted up

The hungry fed
The rich sent away empty.

This is Magnificat.
This is Mary's song.
This is good news.

Intercessory prayers

It's nearly Christmas, God,
the shops and streets are buzzing.
Thank you for this time and space to think and pray.

Be with children everywhere, God, and with their parents:
those who are in danger, those who are hungry,
those who are happy and well-fed.
Loving God,
be their hope and strength.

Be with those for whom Christmas is a hard time, a sad time …
Bless them with who and what they need,
and prompt us to be loving and caring.
Loving God,
be their hope and strength.

We pray for those who are sick,
for those who are dying

and those who are being born,
and for all who care for them.
We pray for those who are longing for good news.
Loving God,
be their hope and strength.

We pray for ourselves, our hopes, our needs, our dreams.
Let your face shine on us, God, on us and on all your world. Amen

Closing responses

In cities and villages,
in tents and tower-blocks,
Jesus is waiting to be born.

In private hospitals,
in refugee camps,
Jesus is waiting to be born.

In us, in our neighbours,
in the world we live in,
Jesus is waiting to be born.

Blessing

Trinity of loving,
our end and our beginning,
let your face shine on us,
let your love be born in us,
bless us with new life.
Amen

Ruth Burgess

As we wait

A response for the four Sundays of Advent Words and music by Joan Reppert

Words and music © Joan Reppert

As we wait for the gift of the Christ child,
as we pray for the ways we can give,
let us light this candle of *faith**,
and live as God wants us to live.

* hope, love, joy

Joan Reppert

Be with us, God

Be with us, God,
in stone stillness
and quiet corners.
**Help us to be lights in the darkness,
lights that burn bravely
in the circle of your love.**

Hear our prayers, God,
our yearnings, our carings,
our concerns, our questions.
**Help us to be lights in the darkness,
lights that burn bravely
in the circle of your love.**

Be in us, God,
in our work, our calling,
our journeys, our wondering.
**Help us to be lights in the darkness,
lights that burn bravely
in the circle of your love.**

Ruth Burgess

Watching and waiting

Be still (Psalm 37)

Wait.

Just wait.
God waits too.
God waits for me to wait.

Empty words.
A barren wilderness.

Waiting in a silence that is the absence of sound,
for there is nothing to hear.
Nothing to see,
nothing to taste, or touch or feel.

Waiting.
Silently waiting.

A barren nothingness.
Waits silently.

Nothing.
Inner nothing.
Outer nothing.

But in this empty barren nothingness …
seeds the Life of the
God who comes.

June McAllister

Watching and waiting

It's not always
a blinding light
that drives
us
to our knees,

it is sitting in
the dark
comforting
a scared child;

it's not always
a burning bush
calling us
to take off
our shoes
and listen,
it is jumping
into a pool
of frigid water
for a charity;

it's not always
cherubim flitting
about the rafters
of a cathedral
as a mighty
voice
speaks,
it is the silence
as we catch
the tears of a
mourning mother
in our hearts;

not every
call
comes with a
capital

C

Thom M Shuman

Winter's wisdom
(an Advent invitation to foolish waiting)

An invitation offered,
a time to pause.
To keep watch,
to wait,
and wait some more.

We are not so good at the waiting.
And waiting again and again seems so foolish.

The world may call us fools,
but we wait,
and wait again.

Every year we repeat the waiting.

Every year we see Christ born again
in our lives and in our world.

Fiona van Wissen

Advent again

Advent
again
telling me to be still
and listen
and let go
and wonder.

I'll try, God.
I want to.

I want love.
I want life.

Ruth Burgess

Know that I am God (Psalm 46)

You are the darkness – descending deep
emptying
filling
your Word to keep.
So silent
so dark
overwhelmed and blind,
I am held in a love
caressing heart and mind.

Yearning and longing –
to love and be loved.
No words can explain
this fire – this pain.

The empty
the absence,
the searching in vain.

I wait.
I surrender.

Your Life to gain.

June McAllister

The light time and the dark time

God of Advent and of waiting times,
we know both darkness and light.
We live with it and in spite of it,
and we give you thanks for the gifts of the night-time and the daytime,
the light time and the dark time. Amen

Fiona Barker

The bogey-god

Afraid you would
smack my knuckles
with a ruler, I
kept my hands
clasped
behind my back,
and so
you could not
fill them with
grace;

certain you were
looking for me so
you could scream
about all the mess
in the kitchen, I
quivered behind
the door, hoping
you would not look there,
and so
you could not
gather me up
in your arms
to wipe away my
fears;

taught to believe
you lurk in the
shadows,
prowling around looking
for a way to get in,
I lock all the doors
and windows,
pull the drapes shut,

turn out the lights
and hide under the quilt,
refusing to answer the door,
and so
the invitation to the party
at your house gathers
dust
in the mailbox.

Thom M Shuman

The Spirit broods

The Spirit broods
over the history of God's people,
sending shafts of light
to illuminate the dark.

The promises of God
through the mouths
of the prophets
ignite a welcome spark.

Long years of darkness
and wilderness wanderings
waiting and watching
for the Messiah to come.

Who could foresee
that a new baby crying
proclaims 'God is with us'?
The light has come!'

Elizabeth Clark

In Advent we wait for you

In Advent we wait for you:
God the maker,
Jesus the storyteller,
Holy Spirit of life.

In Advent we cry to you:
God of Justice,
Jesus of Bethlehem,
Holy Spirit of Hope.

In Advent we long for you.
You, God, are our love,
our warmth,
our light.

Ruth Burgess

Evening service

I come here hoping to find light.
Not everyday light, and yet nothing else:
sometimes this light opens, and becomes deeper –
as much deeper than this as this is deeper than a picture.

With depth comes cold,
as if a door had opened on a mountain;
the space becomes immense,
and yet contained in the same walls.

Most often prayer releases the unfolding;
sometimes reflection on the silver dish,
by the soft, flaring light it makes;
sometimes a spoken word.

There is no hiding here:
light floods my most secret burials,

and the cold stings raw thoughts –
but I am welcome, welcome, welcome.

This, I believe, is part of what it means
to say 'the Holy Spirit';
what fills the spaces between touching points
fluid, and resonant.

Certainly this is what I mean now
when we pray together:
Do not take your Holy Spirit from us.
What would be left?

Only a patch of flesh
in a flat image;
only imagining a self that reached
into the air above the snow.

Roddy Cowie

Hoping and yearning

Advent,
winter days of longing.
Hoping for justice,
yearning for light.

You come,
with warm tears and laughter,
telling the truth,
sharing our lives.

Thank you,
thank you for Advent,
thank you for mystery,
thank you for life.

Ruth Burgess

Bearers of hope

Living God,
help us to be bearers of hope;
to bring your love to those who despair,
to see the possibilities for change
even in the darkest experiences.

May we encourage
reconciliation, healing and justice;
and where our hope is weak,
grant us the courage to wait in the dark
until your light breaks through.
Amen

Chris Polhill

We come expecting nothing

We come expecting nothing
for we have been in this place
many times before
and we know the routine:
we will sit and listen and sing
and then we will go home again.

We expect nothing,
yet part of us – a small part
deep within us –
expects something amazing
expects to be astonished
expects to be awestruck
because part of us
still expects to meet God
and expects the unexpected.

And however many times our
hopes have been dashed, our faith shaken

and our belief in the goodness of the world betrayed
we still hope that today
here in this place
we will meet the living God
we will be touched and moved
we will hear something that
we have not heard before
and our hearts will sing with joy
though we may not understand why
and our burdens will be lifted
as into our darkness and loneliness
God breaks through with an eternal message
to each one of us:
we are loved
we are important
we matter.

And because of this
we will re-orientate our lives
to understand others' needs,
for though the God who calls us to love
may be hidden from our sight,
our neighbours can be seen clearly
and we can love them
for they too are precious in God's sight.

John Butterfield

For you we wait

God of truth
For you we wait

God of justice
For you we wait

God of loving kindness
For you we wait

We know that you are always near.

Ruth Burgess

We will watch and we will wait

Leader: We will watch and we will wait,
A: with the poor and the oppressed,
B: with all who yearn for justice.

Leader: We will watch and we will wait,
A: with the sick and with the dying,
B: with all who long for healing.

Leader: We will watch and we will wait,
A: with the lost and those in darkness,
B: with all who hope for freedom.

Leader: We will watch and we will wait,
All: **for seen or unseen we know that God is present.**

Chris Polhill

We are waiting

For four readers

A: For the Brussel sprouts to cook,
B: for the decorations to come out,
A: for the tree to go up,
B: for the sales in the shops,
A and B: we are waiting.

C: For the light to gather,
D: for the time to pause,
C: for the universe to hold its breath,
D: for the stars to slide,
C and D: we are waiting.

A: For the holidays to come,
B: for the concerts to hear,
A: for the parties to attend,
B: for the children to write their Santa lists,
A and B: we are waiting.

C: For the baby to quicken,
D: for the travellers to arrive,
C: for the angels to clear their throats,
D: for shepherds to hear the singing,
C and D: we are waiting.

A: For the prophets to be fulfilled,
B: for the promise to be believed,
C: for the Word to be spoken,
D: for Incarnation,
All: we are waiting.

Spill the Beans

Blue Christmas

Bring it all to me
(A service for the longest night)

Notes:

You will need a small tree, placed centrally, and enough stars to hang on the tree for everyone. Have some spares near the tree in case people want to hang more than one. You could use an alternative action to tying a star on the tree, e.g. lighting a candle, building a cairn of stones, making a paper chain from strips of coloured paper ...

Suitable songs: appropriate Christmas carols, ancient and modern

Call to worship:

Tonight we gather
with friends and with strangers.
We come as we are to God.

Tonight we gather
with hopes and with questions.
We come as we are to God.

Tonight we gather
with doubts and with dreaming.
We come as we are to God.

Tonight we come as we are to God.
And God has promised to meet us here.

Song

Prayer of approach:

God, it's nearly Christmas –
the restaurants are full of turkey,
the radio is full of carols,
the shops are emptying of stuff.
We remember tonight
the Christmas story:

how you came as a baby,
how you know
what human life is like.

God, hear us:
we come seeking healing for ourselves and others,
we come looking for forgiveness,
we come looking for love.

Meet us, God,
in the words of the Bible,
in the words and lives of our neighbours;
meet us and hold us in love. Amen

Song

Readings (some or all):

Psalm 107

Some people wandered in the desert,
where there were no roads,
and could not find their way
to a city to live in.
They were hungry and thirsty;
they had given up hope.
In the midst of their trouble
they cried out to God.

John 11

Mary came to where Jesus was and she said to him:
'Jesus, if you had been here, my brother would not have died!'
Jesus saw her weeping and he saw how the people with her
were also weeping, and he was deeply moved.
'Where have you buried him?' Jesus asked them.
'Come and see,' they answered.
Jesus wept.
'See how much he loved him,' the people said.

Psalm 130

From the depths of my despair
I call to you, God.
Hear my cry.
If you kept a record of the things I've done wrong
I would have no hope.
But you forgive me and love me.
In your word I trust.

Matthew 11

Jesus said, 'Come to me all of you who are tired of carrying heavy loads, and I will give you rest.'

An invitation:

God knows us.

God knows what delights us, what makes us smile, what makes us sad.

In the next song (you can find the words on the service sheet) God tells us – you can bring me everything.

You were given a star when you came in.

You are invited now to listen to the song and when it is over to come and tie a star onto the tree, as a symbol of placing yourselves and those you love into God's safekeeping.

Song:

'Bring it all to me', Stephen Fischbacher and Suzanne Butler, Fischy Music, on the CD of same name, www.fischy.com

Bring it all to me

Anything excited, anything inspired
bring it all, bring it all to me
everything that's lazy, everything that's tired
bring it all, bring it all to me

Anything that rages, anything that screams
bring it all, bring it all to me
everything that wonders, everything that dreams
bring it all, bring it all to me

You can bring me anything
you can bring me everything
just bring it all, bring it all to me

Anything that's easy, anything that's hard
bring it all, bring it all to me
everything that's perfect, everything that's scarred
bring it all, bring it all to me.

Anything you're proud of, anything you're not
bring it all, bring it all to me
everything you're hiding, everything you've got
bring it all, bring it all to me

You can bring me …

I know how you feel, because I know you
I know how you feel, because I made you

Anything that matters, anything that's real
bring it all, bring it all to me
everything you treasure, everything you feel
bring it all, bring it all to me
everything you treasure, everything you feel
bring it all, bring it all to me

You can bring me …

(Quiet music while people hang stars on the tree.)

Readings (some or all):

Matthew 5

Happy are those who mourn,
God will comfort them.
Happy are those who are kind to others,
God will be kind to them.
Happy are those who work for peace,
God will call them his children.

Psalm 23

God is my shepherd;
I have everything I need.
God gives me new strength
and guides me along the right paths.
When I go through the darkness
God is with me.
I am safe.
God will be with me all my life.
God's house will be my home.

Revelation 21

God's home is for everyone. God will live with everybody.
God will wipe away the tears from their eyes.
Death and pain, grief and crying will be no more.
Anyone who is thirsty will be able to drink the water of life.
God is the first and the last, the end and the beginning.
God can be trusted.

Song

Blessing:

May God bless us this night with hope and with justice.
May those we care about be held in God's love.

May Jesus bless us this night with light and with courage.
May we know that Jesus loves us and he always will.

May the Holy Spirit bless us tonight with tears and with laughter.
May we know the warmth and wonder of God's healing love.
Amen

Sending:

Walk well your way
in the company of the Trinity.
You are God's friends and family,
tonight
and all your nights and days.
Amen

Ruth Burgess, Spill the Beans

Homecoming

You welcome
all
who have
had every door
slammed in their
face:
poverty's children,
streetwalkers,
cleaners of our hotel bathrooms,
asylum seekers,
Ebola carriers;
and then,
you even embrace
us,
who seem
to have difficulty
opening our hearts
to anyone.

Thom M Shuman

The longest night

Come, God of compassion,
to be with all
whose loneliness
makes every night
longer than the
one before;

come, God of brokenness,
to mend those
whose shattered
lives seem impossible
to put back together;

come, God of hungry hearts,
to companion the
people sitting at
one-chair tables
in restaurants overflowing
with parties, and
in apartments with
scarred linoleum floors;

come, God of the gentle arms,
to cuddle
all the children
who cry themselves
to sleep;

come, God of every moment,
come, God of every person,
that we might be
the people others
need to find
in every moment
of their lives.

Thom M Shuman

Until the light comes again

O my God,
when the dark clouds gather over me,
when my spirits are low,
when my body mocks me,
when my heart is closed to the love of your people,
when my eyes are closed to the beauty of your creation –
then, Lord, let me feel your arms around me
until the light comes again.

Andrew Foster

Companion

Where can I go from your spirit? Or where can I flee from your presence?
Psalm 139:7

I've gone into
every dive,
run by despair;

I've wandered
down doubt's
shadowed valleys;

I've locked
every door in my
heart,
and shuttered
every window
in my soul, yet
you
have not
left my side

(even once).

Thom M Shuman

Bring your peace, Lord

Words & music by David MacGregor

Words and music © David MacGregor 2015, Willow Publishing

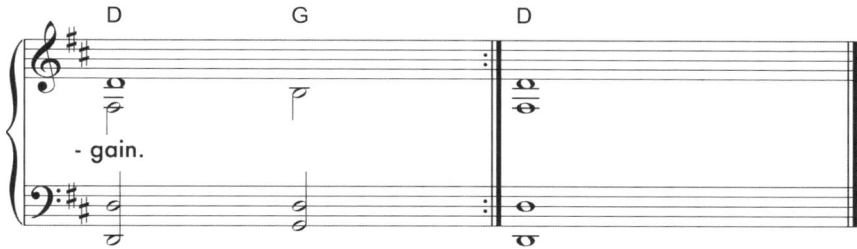

Bring your peace, Lord.
Bring your peace, Lord.
Bring your peace, O Lord –
peace again.
Peace in the hard times,
peace in the pain.
Bring your peace, O Lord –
peace again.

2. Bring your hope, Lord …
3. Bring your love, Lord …
4. Bring your life, Lord …

Note: 'Be our …' can be used instead of 'Bring your …', e.g. 'Be our peace, Lord …'

David MacGregor

A liturgy of remembering

You will need a table with a large central candle/the Christ candle, four small candles and lots of tea-lights (enough for everyone) placed on it, with a Christmas tree, or branch, placed nearby.

As people arrive they are given a small card with a string attached to it (for hanging the card on the tree). During the liturgy, folk are invited to write the name of a loved one who is deceased, or the name of another loss weighing on their heart, or a concern, on the card, and to hang it on the Christmas tree or branch.

Naming our losses:

We name our losses before God:
the loss of a partner in life,
the loss of a family member,
the loss of a friend,
the loss of a loved one,
the loss of a pet,
the loss of health,
the loss of a cherished dream,
the loss of independence,
the loss of self-confidence …

We name our own particular losses in silence before God:
moments of memory – the good ones and the hard ones,
reflecting on the feelings that have been ours in loss.

We pause and remember and reflect *(a time of silence)* …

Lighting the Christ candle:

We now light the Christ candle, a symbol of peace to all on earth;
and we remember all who yearn for a word from God,
all who gaze into the night sky in longing and in hope,
all who listen for an angel song.
As we light this candle we remember
the promise of hope that the Messiah would bring

and we pray that this light would also kindle
a flame of hope within our own hearts.

Light central Christ candle.

Sung response: 'Don't be afraid', John L. Bell and Graham Maule, from *Come All You People*, Wild Goose Publications

Lighting the candle in memory of our loss:

We light this candle in memory of our loss.
We remember and acknowledge the loss and sorrow that brings us here
and we light this candle in memory.
We remember those we have loved,
we remember all we have lost.
We remember in sorrow and in hope.

As we light this candle we remember and acknowledge our loss.

Light candle from the central candle.

Sung response

Lighting the candle of compassion and community:

We light this candle in honour of the love and support
that we have received from family and friends
who have walked with us through the dark valleys in our lives.
We remember their friendly faces, their warm embraces
and the empathy of their presence and we thank you, Holy God,
knowing that their love and support
is also an expression of your love for us.

As we light this candle
we remember the compassion and the gift of those
who have walked with us.

Light candle from central candle.

Sung response

Lighting the candle of wisdom:

We light this candle as a prayer for wisdom.
We know that we cannot change what has befallen, but we can pray
for the wisdom of acceptance and the grace
that would enable us to move forward.
And though in our hearts we may rage against our loss and our pain,
the reality is that we must accept it for healing to begin.

As we light this candle
we pray for wisdom that will lead to the peace that passes understanding.

Light candle from central candle.

Sung response

Lighting the candle of faith:

We light this candle as a symbol of our faith.
Even though we walk through the dark valleys,
we know, we trust, we believe that God walks with us.
And so we light this candle to proclaim our faith
and as a reminder of the hope, peace and love
that God promises to each and every one of us.
As we light this candle we remember God's unending love for us all.

Light candle from central candle.

Sung response

Placing our symbols and the lighting of a small candle:

You are now invited to bring forward your names and concerns and to hang them on the tree (branch), and then to light a candle.

Prayer of grace (following action):

**Gracious God, we remember our pain
and we remember our sorrow.
We have placed these symbols
and lit these candles in memory,**

in honour and in hope.
God of all compassion,
we pray that your Spirit would uphold us.
When we wander through the deep darkness,
help us to see the light of your love,
give us a sense of your presence
that we might know that you are with us yet,
just as you have promised to be.
Lift us above our present sorrow
into the peace of your presence.
In Jesus' name we pray. Amen

Prayers of intercession:

God of the ages,
all around us we see the lights of Christmas,
we hear the sounds of joyful celebration;
at times, we struggle with how to respond.

As the nights have grown longer,
sadness and emptiness, loneliness and pain
wrap around the hearts of many of us, Eternal God.
We aren't always able to put into words
that which causes us to feel melancholy rather than joy.

And so we turn to you, O God, with all of our pain,
and lay it at your feet:
for some, a loved one has died;
for others, a friend has moved away;
others have lost a job, a cherished dream, or a sense of hope.
Some of us are feeling worried, trapped, insecure, adrift or alone.
Some of us are grieving what might have been but will not be,
or grieving over what used to be, but cannot be any more.
Most of us are in need of a place of quiet and calm
in the midst of this busy season.

Whatever it was that has brought us here,
we offer it to you, Mighty God –
you, who were born frail and innocent in Bethlehem's stable –

that we might know of your great and unending love.
We know that there is no pain that does not echo in your heart, O God,
and no joy that does not come from your hand.
We trust that through all the shadows of this world
there yet shines the Light of your Love.

In our darkness, and in the darkness of this world,
may your light continue to shine,
bringing peace, bringing hope, bringing strength and love
to us and to all in need.
We pray
in the name of Jesus Christ Emmanuel,
who is God-with-us. Amen

The Lord's Prayer

Hymn: 'Silent night'

Blessing and sending forth:

We return to the world from which we came:
a world that needs to hear God's words of hope, of peace and of love.

We pray that God, who leads by a Star,
will bring us to the place where the Hope of the World is born,
where the Light of the nations shines bright
and where the Prince of Peace will come to reign.

May we know the gift of love this Christmastime and always.
Amen

Barbara Miller

Time to remember

Introduction:

Everyone is given a cardboard luggage tag as they arrive, on to which they can write the name of a loved one they want to remember. During the service folk will be invited to come forward and hang this on a prayer tree, which should be in an easily accessible location.

Words of welcome:

When the season draws deeper
and the darkness stretches over the day,
the sun lingers longer on the world's other side each morning
and departs quicker in the twilight shadows of evening,
we seek a word of promise that is not caught by the light,
but waits for us anyway.

When the stars seem older and the night longer,
the cold deeper and the colours bluer,
then the season comes to a head
and at the night's longest point
we listen out for the breaking in of the light,
strengthening as it pulls back the darkness
to reveal the promise.

When the memories that accompany us
make the season less merry
and shake some of the meaning away,
then we hold on to them amidst your words of care and grace
nurturing the life within us,
holding us firmly even in the darkness
and accompanying us through this time.

Song

Opening prayer:

Loving God,
who waits with us and walks beside us,
who speaks into all memory and shares every thought,
wait with us now, making this moment precious and close.
Help us lose ourselves in you:
in the depth of love that is generous enough to hold us,
strong enough to wrap us,
eternal enough to call us and patient enough to accompany us.

So may we find the richness of this time,
the wealth of memory and value of story,
the certainty of promise,
the healing of laughter,
the generosity of time.
May we find what we need to find,
know what we need to know
and trust what we need to trust in you.
So be it.
Amen

Reading:

This verse is from William Penn:

'They that love beyond the world cannot be separated by it. Death cannot kill what never dies, nor can spirits ever be divided that love and live in the same divine principle; the root and record of their friendship. If absence be not death, neither is theirs.

Death is but crossing the world, as friends do the seas; they live in one another still. For they must needs be present, that love and live in that which is omnipresent.

This is the comfort of friends, that though they may be said to die, yet their friendship and presence live on in the best sense, ever present, because their memory is immortal. We think not that our friend is lost when they go to another room, nor even if they travel to a distant land and into another world no one is gone. For heaven, that God has created, and this world are all one.'

Song

Readings: Isaiah 25:8–9, John 6:37–40

Prayer for the seasons and lighting of candles:

Place four candles on a tray on a central table.

God of love,
today we share with you our feelings and our thoughts,
at a time when our sense of loss is strong,
when we recognise that this season will not be the same
as it has been in years past,
because that special person who has journeyed with us
does so now only in our memories.
As we admit this to you today,
we bring to you our grief and hurt,
and ask that you make your presence felt as you accompany us.

As the year turns, and seasons come and go, we think of our loved ones:

In the spring, defiant green shoots
break through the dark earth to show us signs of life
and the season of birth is upon us.
We think of those we loved and we think of those we have lost.
So we light this candle for those we loved in spring.

Light first candle (a green candle)

In the summer, the golden sunlight warms us,
the blue skies lift our spirits,
and the season of growth is upon us.
We think of those we loved and we think of those we have lost.
So we light this candle for those we loved in summer.

Light second candle (a yellow candle)

In the autumn, the trees turn gold and red and rich brown,
and the season of fruits and harvest is upon us.
We think of those we loved and we think of those we have lost.
So we light this candle for those we loved in autumn.

Light third candle (a red or gold candle)

In the winter, the world turns white, the earth sleeps,
and the season of rest is upon us.
We think of those we loved and we think of those we have lost.
So we light this candle for those we loved in winter.

Light fourth candle (a white candle)

Time passes.
The cycle of birth and growth and fruit and sleep continues.
Time heals and memories sustain.
We do not get over our loss, yet we do find a new normal:
a new way of living without those we held so dear.

We pray today for those who grieve.
We pray today for those whom we remember.
We pray today for all our loved ones:
brothers and sisters,
husbands and wives,
parents and children,
friends and companions,
that we each may find our way in this world
and be reunited with those we love
in spirit and in grace in the next.
Amen

Symbolic activity:

People are invited to bring their tags forward and to place them on the tree, quiet music playing as they do so.

Concluding thoughts:

We have remembered.
We have been still.
We have given support to each other.
We have received strength from God.

Our loved ones are freed from the chains of life on earth
to the liberty of their heavenly lives.
One day we will all be together,
united by our love for each other and our love for God.
Until that day we leave them in the care of the Creator,
the Saviour and the Inspirer:
God Almighty, Father, Son and Holy Spirit.

Song

Blessing:

May God bless us
and heal us
and hold us in love
today, tonight
and for evermore. Amen

Julie Rennick, Spill the Beans

Christmas doesn't work for everyone

Christmas doesn't work for everyone,
does it, God?

For a lot of people Christmas is sad
and full of bad memories.

For a lot more Christmas is cold
and hungry, and lonely.

Help us, God, to watch and to listen:
to watch out for people who might need our help,
to listen to people who tell us their stories.

And even though it's Advent
and we're supposed to be watching and listening,
it's OK to act too,
when that's what's needed.

It's OK to cry
and to talk about sad stuff
and to love and listen.

It's OK to give someone cash for their meter
or food for their table.
It's good to share our resources.

Christmas doesn't work for everyone,
does it, God?

But it might work a bit better
if we looked for You
in the people around us,
as well as in the manger.

Ruth Burgess, Spill the Beans

Winter in December

A thanksgiving for winter

God of beauty and grace,
we thank you for all that winter brings to us,
for revealing the stark beauty of a tree's outline
and giving the wonder and intricacy of a flake of snow.

We thank you for a time to rest from mowing the lawn
or from weeding the vegetable bed;
a time to expectantly plan what seeds to plant in the season to come,
but from the comfort of a cosy chair.

We delight in playing in the snow,
or at least in the hope that we might.
We thank you for long dark nights when we can watch the moon rise
or appreciate the bright company of stars.

We welcome the goose, the teal and the fieldfare
as they visit our winter shores and woods,
and the snowdrop as it interrupts bleak January days with delicate beauty.

We thank you for cold wintry walks
when we can snuggle into our favourite scarf,
look forward to a hot cup of tea in our hands
and reminisce in front of the fire.

We even thank you for those grey and wet mild days,
when the cold does not bite
and we have a topic of conversation to take with us through the day.

Grant us the graciousness to see winter's gifts
and enjoy earth's quiet season.

Simon Taylor

Solstice

Solstice, and the garlic must be planted,
each clove deep within the earth.
Lost, until its summer worth
rises, rejoicing in new life new granted.

Solstice and the darkness seems our friend,
a time for yule fires, company,
wassail and gentle liberty,
as if the celebrations need not end.

Solstice and the sun at each day's dawn
comes earlier with the growing light,
scattering the clouds of night,
thanksgiving that another year is born.

Solstice and we come to you once more
thanking you for what has been,
certain that you will redeem
the earth, and all its majesty restore.

The solstice skies are grey, the air's damp haze
penetrates our coats and blurs the sight
of we who trudge toward the stable light,
hope's inspiration in these darkling days.

Yet hope, though hiding, with the season grows
as mornings warm and each dawn chorus cheers,
and fragile faith, long battered by the years,
will be renewed; for as the yule log glows,

old tales are told, old friends received with pleasure,
the simple truths, which are not subject to
the turning year, will fill the hearts of those
who raise a glass to toast Love beyond measure,

not limited within a Christmas story
but freed beyond this night's star-scattered glory.

Brian Hick

Seeking silence

Where do you go to find silence,
to listen closely,
to seek winter's deep stillness?

Draw winter's shawl around your shoulders,
wrap yourself in the soothing darkness,
feel the embrace of God's love.

Find comfort in hidden places,
know you need not fear the dark.

Seek the wisdom of the season:
the unseen roots deep underground, the bulbs, the tiny seeds,
waiting with infinite patience,
waiting with hidden hope.

Honour the winter dormancy of your soul.

Give yourself permission to wait and be still,
no need to rush,
no need to rush …

Wait in the darkness.
Hold tight to the promise.

New hope will come
with the tender green beauty of spring.

Fiona van Wissen

The heavens declare

The heavens declare the glory of God; the skies proclaim the work of his hands.
(Psalm 19:1, NIV)

Unlike most people, and being well aware that to some it just appears downright strange, I look forward to winter.

It isn't because, having been brought up on the island of Arran, I enjoy the tempest sea as it undergoes some kind of catharsis brought on by a south-westerly gale, though I confess that does hold a great attraction for me.

But it is more because I can see with greater clarity the night sky on a cold clear night, and have longer to view it than during the other seasons of the year.

That sense of awe that you experience at the end of an eyepiece of a telescope is present – when you consider the relative size of our planet within the solar system, set in our galaxy, amidst the vastness of space that is our universe.

I can spend hours in the quiet of the night, oblivious to the cold weather around me. And there comes a point when it is as if there is no telescope any more, just myself alone in the universe.

It's a unique experience but also very hard to explain in words.

Gordon MacLeod

Winter in Dunblane

9am.
Winter sun, rising
between bare branches,
dazzles my eyes.

Hungry sparrows
look for breakfast,
crows and jackdaws
cross the sky.

Advent:
time to watch and wonder,
to ask God questions,
to hear God cry.

Ruth Burgess

Midwinter on Ulva
'We have come, following a star'

Here we are, God, on a grey midwinter day, with a gale blowing up;
we've risked a ferry crossing and walked through the mud to be here:
we must be slightly mad – who could ever mistake us for wise men?
And yet, God of holy fools, we have come
Following a star.

Here we are, God, in the middle of celebrating Christmas:
time with family, reaching out to friends, blessings of giving and receiving,
decorated homes, party food and a feast of carols:
yet now, God of joyful celebration, we have come
Following a star.

Here we are, God, in a world of confusion and injustice
trying to understand what is happening in politics, the economy;
anxious, angry and fearful, asking 'Where is God in all this?'
Right now, God of hard questions, we have come
Following a star.

Here we are, God, in an island apart, amid quiet and changeful beauty;
at the turning of the year, the days already getting longer,
light glinting on the leaves of holly and ivy, rain nourishing the earth,
bulbs growing underground, signs of new life to come.
Yes, God of creation's mystery, we have come
Following a star.

We have come to listen to an ancient story, to wonder at its meaning,
to sing much-loved carols, to care for each other, to pray for the world,
to bring our gift of worship, and to put ourselves in your hands
as we travel on.
God who welcomes us, we have come
Following a star.
Amen

Jan Sutch Pickard

Long for home

Short dark days
logs piled high
chimneys blaze
hot mince pie.

Ice-cold toes
sun hangs low
dripping nose
north winds blow.

Breath that steams
slipping feet
children's dreams
toys and treats.

Once was mud
frosty rut
twisted ankle
stagger strut.

Snowflakes float
earth is under
white frock coat
crystal wonder.

Autumn nailed
to a cross
death has failed
there's no loss.

Soul storms rage
waters foam
sailors age
long for home.

Christ redeems
winter starts
truth and dreams
healed in hearts.

Stuart Barrie

Longest night

On winter's longest night
ebony stillness unfurls
a field of cosmic sequins
incomparably vast,
flung out sparkling,
granulated from some
mass of stuff
long since exploded.

I ponder galaxies,
each embracing
a hundred billion
shining
suns.

My mind stumbles
in this darkness,
but catches itself
on the solid joy
of living in this galaxy,
whirling around
this little sun,
grateful for firm grasp
of infinitesimal smallness,
expansive as the universe
on winter's longest night.

Bonnie Thurston

When the snow falls deep

When the snow falls deep
I fall too,
on purpose.

Then I move my arms and legs
down and up
and up and down.

Lying there
I can see the sun –
it's dazzling,
bouncing off snow crystals
dancing all around me

My next move
is the tricky one.
Somehow I have to get up
without disturbing
any more snow
or smudging my wings.

When I'm ready
I will do it very carefully
and uncommonly slowly.
Tonight more snow may come
or wind or rain
or heavy feet
or bright bright stars.

But until then
you'll be able to see
where I met God
and God met me
and we made
a new snow angel.

Ruth Burgess

Winter praises

I pull open the curtains in the warm kitchen –
glorious gold streaks
beneath the puffed pink snow clouds
open my sleep-filled eyes
to this late sunrise.

Outside the house, breadcrumbs
skitter on the thin ice
that crackles as the blackbird lands.
Later, searching his share,
a robin taps against the glass door.

Hot porridge,
toast with butter
and my fourth cup of tea,
a second sweater,
my ear-muffed furry hat,
double socks and walking boots.
I'm ready
to fetch the paper
in the sharp bright air.

Rooks are circling above
their giant sycamore mansion,
its profile strong, stark, bare,
like the men who once worked here
who now are buried in the hard earth
they tilled or mined.
Winter for them was harsh,
bitter, cruel, biting
as they toiled for food and fires and lighting.

Winter flowers have special beauty:
rising from bare frosted ground,
aconites to surprise us,
snowdrops, well-named,
delicate green-white bells hanging in the snow,

early hellebores, the Christmas roses,
bright yellow jasmine on the garden wall.

Low winter sunshine
gilds and blinds us on the road at 3pm.
The wide sky is palest blue;
soft grey-mauve clouds
turn pink, then fiery,
before the dark of evening overtakes them.

Liz Gregory-Smith

Winter shore walk

Tired and hungry for beauty
I stood at your window.
Arran presented herself proud and radiant.
Goatfell glinted snow.

We pulled on boots to walk
and crossed the golf course,
the frozen grass crunching comfortably
beneath our feet.

On the beach
the sand was rigid in patches,
crystallised in ice.

Gulls, swooping and soaring,
echoed the sea's screaming energy.

Swathes of colour:
blues, reds, peaches, whites
ribboned the grey sky.

I gulped the cold air greedily,
cramming my lungs to hurting point
and breathed out laughter.

Mary Hanrahan

The light shines

The light shines in the darkness, and the darkness did not overcome it.
John 1:5

Jesus spoke to them, saying, 'I am the light of the world. Whoever follows me will never walk in darkness but will have the light of life.'
John 8:12

Jesus said, 'I came that they may have life, and have it abundantly.'
John 10:10b

In the late '50s my family moved to a farm with no mains electricity or gas. Although the number of appliances available was minute compared with today, we had been used to a gas stove and boiler (for washing clothes), vacuum, iron, wireless, gramophone and TV. However, by far the biggest loss was electric light. I hated doing my homework by oil lamp. It was hot, smoky, smelly and dirty. It made my head ache and didn't even give a good light.

Going to bed by candlelight was even worse. Apart from the low level of light, the flame flickered, cast menacing shadows and, in an old draughty house, blew out at the most inconvenient moments. Even now, so many years later, I still feel a sense of wonder and thanksgiving that I can walk into a room, flick a switch and, instantaneously, the room is filled with light.

While I appreciate that dancing candle flames are beautiful and can speak of Christ, the Light of the world, for me the clean, clear, odourless electric light is a better symbol of the one who came to give life – and to give it abundantly.

Pamela Whyman

Kinharvie walk

Torn two ways.
Workshop junkie …
loving the buzz and laughter,
yearning to share.

Quiet voice within
saying solitude is what you need.
Be still. Face yourself …
and Me.

I listened, said my goodbyes
and stepped out …
into heavy frost
silence
and cattle and sheep grazing the frozen grass,
their easy calm movements
reflecting a rhythm of life we daily violate
with our schedules, timetables and clocks.
Yet how easily we recover its simplicity
in a few deep refreshing breaths.

I walked and wondered …
at frost on ferns,
at filigreed fronds of silvered grasses,
at bare branches black against a winter sky,
at red berries, red-breasted robins
and the breathtaking grandeur of a kestrel hovering.

I 'stood and stared' …
at convoluted patterns in icy puddles,
at the half-hidden depths
in woods dark and enticing.

Alone in a winter Eden, yet never lonely.
My spirit sang within and brimmed onto lips.
Walking, singing, praising.
Every step a new revelation
of creation's variety and gleeful spontaneity.

I returned, energised, renewed, to lunch and people,
glowing with exercise and joy.
A fuller, better person to share.

Mary Hanrahan

The sense of winter

The light shines in the darkness.
John 1:5

I will give you treasures of darkness.
Isaiah 45:3

The light is more precious in winter,
being in short supply.
Out of the enveloping darkness
we emerge
to grasp with eager hands
the chilled brightness, briefly,
honouring its soon passing.

The low sun,
illuminating deep-down hidden things,
shining into dark corners,
hurting our eyes,
all too soon slips below the horizon
and the darkness rolls in
and over
and around.

But, but
there are treasures in darkness,
wild and secret,
undiscovered until touched or tasted,
sight denied.

Winter is a feast for the senses,
winter is darkness.
And light
and darkness …

Carolyn Morris

Winter prayers

Lord, warm my heart this winter.
May I have a fiery coal to put in another's hearth.

We pray for those who cannot easily keep warm,
the housebound whose days seem long.
God of the winter,
Hear our prayer.

I'm excited at the snow.
It's a special gift to break my routine and live for fun.
Thank you.

May all children in our area be able to play in safety.
God of the winter,
Hear our prayer.

I'm stunned at the tall fir trees clothed in their snow mantle.
I praise you for the forests: the life-breath of our environment.

We pray for all who work in forestry and farming.
God of the winter,
Hear our prayer.
Amen

Liz Gregory-Smith

The Lord of the winds

(Tune: 'Back in Dalry', Scots traditional)

The Lord of the winds has whirled his winds on,
roaring from dusk through the night until dawn:
majesty, glory and power are his,
no shame to worship such splendour as this.

Who is the one whose will the winds know,
singing their torrent of praise as they go?
Surely the one who has made all that is:
no shame to worship such splendour as this.

So choose if you will to batten your door:
I will go down through the wind to the shore,
watching the waves break in fury and bliss:
no shame to worship such splendour as this.

Roddy Cowie

Stars

Midnight cold – a Shropshire hillside,
footpaths sodden – thick with mud.
Ten of us from the inner city
rested a while, and stood
looking up, and tracing the pattern
of stars in a night sky, clear
and bright,
aching a little from bodies unused
to country walks at night.
And a boy's voice broke the silence
saying, 'Where are we going then –
are we following these bleeding stars
all the way to Bethlehem?'

Ruth Burgess

Christingle

Three sets of opening responses

A:

It's Christmas Eve.
Wow!

One more sleep and it's Christmas Day.
Wow!

Christmas is getting closer.
Wow!

So let's enjoy Christmas Eve together.
Let's enjoy this special night.

B:

Are you ready to sing some songs?
Yes!

That's the right answer – are you ready to listen to a story?
Yes!

And are you ready to make a Christingle?
Yes!

God is here with us.
Let's help each other sing and smile and pray tonight.

C:

Children and pensioners,
friends and strangers,
We come to God's house.

In good times and bad times,
in light and in darkness,
We come to God's house.

Seeking God's wisdom,
asking God's blessing,
We come to God's house.

We come together in God's house tonight.

Ruth Burgess

A prayer for a Christingle service

As the lit candles on the Christingles light up our faces,
so, loving Jesus, may your light shine into our lives.
Shine brightly in the darkness to bring us security and peace,
to bring us hope and joy.

As the red ribbon surrounds our Christingles,
we thank you, Lord, that you surround us with your love.
Circle us with your care each day and night;
thank you that we are always in your thoughts.

May these Christingles remind us to shine as lights in the world,
bringing hope and joy to those who are in darkness.
May the light of Jesus shine in our hearts so that
we may bring love and peace into our world.
Jesus, Light of the world, bring hope in the darkness.
Amen

Simon Taylor

A story with dressing up

Before the service prepare the following:

- *A bag containing a costume for Mary*
- *A bag containing a costume for Joseph*
- *A bag containing a costume for an innkeeper*
- *A bag containing a costume for Herod*
- *A bag containing costumes for a band of angels (lots of tinsel, etc)*
- *A bag containing costumes for a group of shepherds*
- *Three bags containing costumes for wise people, include a wrapped gift in each bag*
- *A bag containing a baby doll to nurse*
- *Hide a large silver star under a seat/pew.*
- *Have a stage/central area with two people in charge of a manger and a chair for Mary, which are placed onstage at the appropriate time (see below).*
- *Give out the costumes and doll to random individuals as they enter the building. Have a label on each bag asking folk to get dressed up before the service begins, and to leave their costume and bag on their chair at the end of the service. All costumes should be loose-fitting and can involve hats, etc – have fun, be creative.*

Narrator:

As it's Christmas Eve we're going to tell you a Christmas story, and there are some people sitting in the church who are going to help us.

So let's begin the story with a young woman called Mary.

Are you somewhere in the congregation, Mary? Stand up please so we can see you …

Mary was expecting a baby, and she was engaged to a carpenter called Joseph. Can you stand up, Joseph? …

Mary and Joseph went on a long journey from their home to a town called Bethlehem so that they could be counted in a census. So let's ask Mary and Joseph to come up to the front.

Music (30 seconds approximately): one verse of 'In the bleak midwinter'

When Mary and Joseph got to Bethlehem they had to find somewhere to stay. They knocked on lots of doors but everywhere was full up. Then they found an inn on the edge of town, and an innkeeper opened the door. Have we got an innkeeper? … Please come up to the front.

Music: one verse of 'Once in royal David's city'

The innkeeper told Mary and Joseph that there was a stable around the back of the inn where they could stay for the night. Mary and Joseph were relieved. Joseph guessed that Mary's baby might be born that night, and in the stable noticed a manger which would make a good bed for a newborn baby.

A manger? … Thanks … And a chair for Mary? … Thank you.

Mary and Joseph settled down for the night. They were both very tired. And in the middle of the night, Mary's baby was born …

Now, I think someone is nursing the baby? … Could you bring the baby up to the front?

Music: one verse of 'Away in a manger'

Outside Bethlehem, there were some angels who were having a choir rehearsal.

God had asked these angels to sing and give a message to some shepherds who were out on the hills looking after their master's sheep. The angels told the shepherds that a special baby had been born that night: a baby who would bring light to the world, and he would be called Jesus. The angels then told the shepherds to go to Bethlehem and find the baby.

So have we got some angels? … And some shepherds? … Can you come up to the front?

Music: one verse of 'While shepherds watched'

Now, while all this was going on there was something new and bright shining in the sky. What was it now? … I remember: it was a special bright shiny star. So we need a star. We've got one somewhere … Can everyone look under their seats/pews and see if they can find a beautiful shiny star? …

Well done. Can you bring the star up to the front?

Music: one verse of 'Twinkle, twinkle, little star'

Sadly, there's a bad king in this story. Can you whisper his name? … That's right: King Herod.

I'm not sure I ought to do this, but he is part of the story too. If there's a King Herod here, could he come up to the front?

Music: one verse of 'Unto us a boy is born'

After the baby Jesus was born, three wise people arrived at Herod's palace in Jerusalem. Herod listened to them talk about the star leading them to a place where a special baby had been born. Herod didn't want any special babies in his land. He wanted to be the only person who was important in Jerusalem. He asked the wise people to go and find the baby, and to come back and tell him where it was.

We've got some wise people somewhere … Could you come up to the front?

Music: one verse of 'We three kings'

The wise people gave the baby Jesus the presents they'd brought him … and you know they didn't go and tell King Herod about the stable and where Jesus was: they went home another way.

And Mary and Joseph remembered all the visitors who had come to see the baby Jesus. Jesus, born in Bethlehem. The Light of the world.

So Mary, Joseph, innkeeper, manger-and-chair-providers, baby-minder, angels, shepherds, star-keeper, Herod, wise people – thank you for helping to tell our story. Take a bow.

We're going to sing now *(hymn number)* …

Ruth Burgess

Christingle

A story with actions and noise

For this story you need Christmas tree decorations in the shapes of characters in the Nativity story. You could make them out of cardboard or you could purchase them from a website (e.g. Yellow Moon: www.yellowmoon.org.uk).

You need to come up with an action or a noise for each character. We used these:

- Joseph: stroked his beard.
- Mary: circled a hand over her stomach.
- The baby: arms rocked in front of body.
- The donkey: said 'Hee haw'.
- The stable: joined fingertips over its head to make a roof shape.
- The angel: put palms together as in prayer.
- The shepherds: said 'Baaaa'.
- The star: clenched and unclenched its fists and said 'Twinkle, twinkle'.
- The camel tapped with alternate hands on the pew.
- The wise men: pointed at the sky.

Each character stood to make their noise or perform their action.

Decorations were given out as people arrived: families and friends who arrived together were given one decoration to share, those who arrived alone were given a decoration each.

As it's Christmas Eve we're going to tell the Christmas story, and this year we want everybody to join in. Can you find the tree decoration you were given when you came in?

Have a look at which one you've got. It could be MARY or JOSEPH or a CAMEL or a SHEPHERD or a WISE MAN or a STAR or a DONKEY or an ANGEL or a STABLE or the BABY Jesus.

152   Winter

(Explain that each character in the story has an action or a noise: folk do the action, noise when they hear the name of their character; the narrator gives a pause at each name to allow this to happen. Have a practice for each character. Encourage all members of the group to participate.)

So let's begin the story with a young woman who was called MARY. She was expecting a BABY and she was engaged to a carpenter and he was called JOSEPH.

Now, the Christmas story is a story of journeys and MARY and JOSEPH had to go on a long journey from their home in Nazareth to a town called Bethlehem so that they could be counted in the census. Because the journey was so long they probably took with them a DONKEY to help them on their way.

When they got to Bethlehem they had to find somewhere to stay. They knocked on lots of doors but everywhere was full. Then they found another inn on the edge of town and an innkeeper opened the door.

The Innkeeper told MARY and JOSEPH that his inn was full but there was a STABLE around the back of the inn where they could stay. They were pleased. They found the STABLE and unloaded their things from the back of the DONKEY.

Now JOSEPH guessed that Mary's BABY might be born that night and he saw that the STABLE had a manger in it, which would make a good bed for a newborn BABY.

They settled down for the night. They both were very tired. And in the middle of the night Mary's BABY was born. They called him Jesus and they wrapped him up in special cloths and put him in the manger.

Meanwhile, outside Bethlehem there were some ANGELS who were having a choir rehearsal. God had asked these ANGELS to sing and to give a message to some SHEPHERDS who were out on the hills looking after their master's sheep.

The ANGELS told the SHEPHERDS all about the STABLE and what they would find there. So now the SHEPHERDS had to go on a journey from the hills down to Bethlehem and off they went.

They found the STABLE and they saw MARY and JOSEPH and the BABY Jesus and they saw the DONKEY as well. And then the SHEPHERDS went back to the hills to look after the sheep.

Now, while all this was going on, there was something new and bright shining in the sky. What was it now? I remember: it was a special bright shiny STAR.

Do you remember who had been following the STAR? It was some WISE MEN. They had travelled a long, long way from another land. It was too far for them to carry all their clothes and food themselves so they might have brought a CAMEL with them to help them carry everything.

The WISE MEN had been looking for a newborn king and they had gone to look for him in Herod's palace in Jerusalem. Herod had listened to them talk about the STAR leading them to a place where a special BABY would be born. Herod didn't want anyone special in his land. He wanted to be the only person who was important in Jerusalem. He asked the WISE MEN to go and find the BABY and to come back and tell him where it was.

The STAR led the WISE MEN to the STABLE and they tied up their CAMEL outside.

The WISE MEN gave the BABY Jesus the presents they'd brought him, and you know they didn't go and tell King Herod about the STABLE. They went home, with their CAMEL, another way.

Soon after this an ANGEL told JOSEPH to take MARY and the BABY Jesus to another country where they would be safe from danger, and so they travelled with their DONKEY to the land of Egypt.

People still travel today, people still need to leave dangerous places to find a safe place for their children to grow up. This year some families have come from dangerous places to Scotland to find a new safe place to call home. This Christmas Scotland welcomes them.

Thank you for listening to the Christmas story and for joining in. Perhaps when you get home tonight you can colour in your decoration and hang it on your tree.

So, one last time, thank you again to the WISE MEN, the ANGELS, the SHEPHERDS, THE CAMELS, MARY and JOSEPH, THE STARS, DONKEYS, STABLES and BABIES.

The End

Ruth Burgess

Litany of the Christingle

As they enter the church each child is given a bag containing the elements of a Christingle: an orange with a central hole cut at the top for a candle, a red ribbon, 4 cocktail sticks, some dried fruit (raisins, currants) and jelly sweets, a circle of aluminium foil, and a small candle.

You will need:

– Stewards to hand out the Christingle bags

– A worship leader

– A cantor/song leader

– Four element-bearers, with one doubling up as a reader

– A trumpeter (optional – but very much enjoyed)

– An organist/musicians

The song goes to the tune of 'Frère Jacques'. Each line is sung first by the song leader (SL) then repeated by everyone. The words suggest the actions: 'Stand up', 'Sit down', 'Smile at your neighbours', etc. The song leader should be in a visible position, next to the worship leader, and points in the directions from where the elements are processed into the worship space, and demonstrates the actions in the song.

The elements of the Christingle come from four places in the church, from east, north, west and south. The oranges are in a bowl, the ribbons in a basket, the sweets in a wide bowl, and a large candle is carried in a lamp/on a stand, etc. The element-bearers should dress in bright clothing and carry the elements in uplifted hands. The bowl/basket containing each element is brought to a central table, then an orange, a ribbon, etc is delivered to the worship leader. During the litany the worship leader demonstrates how to assemble a Christingle. Make sure all of this movement can be clearly seen from around the space, and practise it before worship.

Note: In a large building, like a cathedral, you might want to include a herald (carrying a decorated staff – a riot of ribbons, baubles and tinsel wrapped round a broomstick) to help focus the movement. The herald comes and accompanies each element-bearer to the central table.

SL: Stand up, stand up
All: Stand up, stand up

SL: Turn around
All: Turn around

SL: From the east come oranges
All: From the east come oranges

SL: Sweet and round
All: sweet and round

> *Trumpet fanfare, then organ music as the oranges are processed into the worship space. After they are brought to the central table, one orange is delivered to the worship leader.*

SL: Sit down, sit down
All: Sit down, sit down

SL: On your seat
All: On your seat

SL: Smile at your neighbours
All: Smile at your neighbours

SL: Stamp your feet
All: Stamp your feet

Words about the orange:

Worship leader:

The orange represents the world: the world held lovingly in God's hands – from the very beginning of time, and every day and every night until forever … Now take your orange out of your bag and hold it gently in the palm of your hand. Think about how fragile the world is … and about ways you can help to take care of it, and everybody who lives upon the planet.

Prayer:

Loving God of us all,
thank you for the whole world,
of which we are just a little part.
Help us to love it and take care of it:
hills and valleys, streams and seas;
places we dream of visiting
and places we know like the back of our hand.
Living God of us all,
thank you for the whole world,
of which we are just a little part.
Help us to love it and take care of it:
birds and beasts, wild things that roam
and pets who are part of the family;
funny-looking creepy-crawlies that swarm and sweep
and group together in their thousands;
fantastic creatures that the world will never see again,
if we don't look after them.
Loving, living God of us all,
thank you for the whole world,
of which we are just a little part.
Help us to love it and take care of it:
people all over the planet –
short and tall, fat and skinny, dark and pale –
you made us all so wonderfully different –
what a thoughtful, creative thing to do.
You have given us family,
next-door neighbours, best friends,
strangers we've never met and aren't likely to;
we've been blessed with people we love and like
and people who get right up our noses.
We're all part of the world
and not one of us is more or less important to you.
Amen

SL: Stand up, stand up
All: Stand up, stand up

Christingle 157

SL: Turn your head
All: Turn your head

SL: From the north come ribbons
All: From the north come ribbons

SL: Bright and red
All: Bright and red

Trumpet fanfare, then organ music as the ribbons are processed into the worship space. After they are brought to the central table, one ribbon is delivered to the worship leader.

SL: Sit down, sit down
All: Sit down, sit down

SL: On your seat
All: On your seat

SL: Wink at your neighbours
All: Wink at your neighbours

SL: Stamp your feet
All: Stamp your feet

Words about the ribbon:

Worship leader:

The red ribbon represents the love of God shown to us in Jesus. With Jesus, there are no exceptions: no one is ever left out, no one forgotten or made to feel unimportant. God's love holds everybody together and we are all one big family.

Now, take out your ribbon and hold it up. Think of all the people in the world who need to be wrapped up in love and care. Now, put your ribbon round your world, and when you do, think of someone special you want to remember: it can be someone who's been on your mind, or it can be people in a place where folk are hungry or hurting. You can say their name or the place out loud, or just whisper it to God. When you have finished, hold your orange up …

SL:	Stand up, stand up
All:	Stand up, stand up
SL:	Turn your feet
All:	Turn your feet
SL:	From the west come raisins
All:	From the west come raisins
SL:	Currants, sweets
All:	Currants, sweets

Trumpet fanfare, then organ music as the fruit and sweets are processed into the worship space. After they are brought to the central table, some fruit and sweets are delivered to the worship leader.

SL:	Sit down, sit down
All:	Sit down, sit down
SL:	On your seat
All:	On your seat
SL:	Wave at your neighbours
All:	Wave at your neighbours
SL:	Stamp your feet
All:	Stamp your feet

Words about the fruits and sweets:

Worship leader:

The fruits and sweets represent the wonderful gifts that God has showered over all the earth.

Take out the fruits and sweets. As you place them on the cocktail stick, like so, think about all the wonderful foods you've eaten – and then turn to your neighbour and tell them what your favourite food is … Think about us sharing the gifts of the earth so that everybody has enough, and how you might be able to help people in the world and in your neighbourhood who are hungry. Talk about that with your neighbour …

We place the fruits and sweets on the four sides of the orange, like this, as a way of remembering that the gifts of the globe are meant for everyone: people in all four corners of God's earth are entitled to food, water, shelter ...

SL: Stand up, stand up
All: Stand up, stand up

SL: Turn round tight
All: Turn round tight

SL: From the south come candles
All: From the south come candles

SL: Burning bright
All: Burning bright

> *Trumpet fanfare, then organ music as the candle is processed into the worship space. After the large candle is brought to the central table, a small unlit candle is delivered to the worship leader. After delivering it, the element-bearer goes to the Reader's lectern.*

SL: Sit down, sit down
All: Sit down, sit down

SL: On your seat
All: On your seat

SL: Blow a kiss at your neighbours
All: Blow a kiss at your neighbours

SL: Stamp your feet
All: Stamp your feet

Words about the candle:

Worship leader:

OK, now to complete your Christingle, first place the aluminium foil into the centre-cut of your orange, like this. Then take your candle and fit it into your orange.

Winter

The candle represents Jesus, the Light of the world. Jesus is the light that shines in the darkness. The light that cannot be put out.

Now hold your finished Christingle high, remembering dark places in the world and people in need of hope.

Now hear some ancient words about Jesus:

Reader: John 1:1–5

SL:	Oranges, ribbons
All:	Oranges, ribbons
SL:	Candles, sweets
All:	Candles, sweets
SL:	Our Christingles
All:	Our Christingles
SL:	Are complete
All:	Are complete
SL:	Stand up, stand up
All:	Stand up, stand up
SL:	Steady now
All:	Steady now
SL:	Turn round slowly
All:	Turn round slowly
SL:	Take a bow
All:	Take a bow

Ruth Burgess and Sally Foster-Fulton

Leftovers

This monologue is for the end of a Christingle service. Props include a broom, dustpan, half-eaten Christingle, etc ... Adapt the wording to your local situation. Speaker enters, holding a broom ...

Time to clear up then.

That's another happy and successful Christingle service over.

Here and there, as always, a few discarded raisins, abandoned oranges and cocktail sticks left on hymnbook ledges, or on the floor *(starts to sweep up)*.

I suppose their owners lost interest once the candles had been blown out and they'd secretly eaten the sweets during the last hymn and closing prayer.

It's a real shame they've not taken them home to enjoy.

Ah, well *(shrugs, then picks up an abandoned Christingle and shows it to the congregation)*.

You know, those Christingles were all fashioned with such care, and now look at it – spoiled. Never mind, the important parts are still there: the orange encircled with a band of red ribbon (well, actually we used sticky tape!) reminds us of God's never-ending love for the world. The candle, too, is still in place – that's to remind us of Jesus, the Light of the world. But then you've been listening and already knew that, didn't you? So I don't really need to say any more.

And yet, when I think about it, those empty cocktail sticks, stripped of their jelly sweets and raisins, could easily be a reminder that in some parts of the world people don't have enough food or all the luxuries that we do. I don't suppose they'd say no to raisins if they were offered them. *(Sweeps up raisins, cocktail sticks, etc; pauses and glances at watch or the clock).*

Ah, it's getting late *(looks towards window)*. It's dark outside. And the wind's blowing up a gale *(appropriate comment on weather)*.

Right, nearly finished, it's been a busy night *(puts aside dustpan and brush)*.

But, you know – I like Christingle services. People always go away with smiles on their faces and it's good to remember that, whatever happens in our lives,

God's love is always there for us.

Well, that's all done for now. I'm off for a nice cup of tea *(picks up coat, scarf and keys and starts to walk away, then pauses and looks back at congregation).*

Same time next year then? *(Exits.)*

Kathy Crawford

Benediction
(for when the Christingle service is held on Christmas Eve)

It's almost time.
Tonight is the night.
Thank God!
Go home you noisy little people.
Sleep tight.
Amen

Ruth Burgess and Sally Foster-Fulton

Early Christmas Eve

There was no room
(Opening responses)

Lord Jesus,
there was no room for you
in the inn on the night that you were born:
Help us to make room in our hearts for you.

Lord Jesus,
a star shone brightly
in the sky to announce your birth:
Lead us to your light that we too may worship you.

Lord Jesus,
angels sang at your birth
filling the night sky with the celebration of divine love:
**Fill us with joy
as we sing the praises of the Christ child
who is God-with-us.**

Simon Taylor

Christmas Eve

Deep within me God lies curled;
his path goes through me to the world:
deep within me God lies curled.

I cannot travel, I must wait;
the way is dark, the hour is late:
I cannot travel, I must wait.

I need a place – where can I turn
to find the help for which I yearn?
I need a place – where can I turn?

I must lie down upon the earth
to bring the God within to birth:
I must lie down upon the earth.

The animals will wait with me,
and share the waiting patiently,
and share the waiting patiently.

And you, my love, will hold the light,
to ease my labour in the night:
and you, O Love, will hold the light.

Now I must take and I must give,
breathe in and out, that He may live:
now I must take and I must give.

A song will sound, a star will shine.
I give Him birth who gave me mine:
a song will sound, a star will shine.

Sue Sabbagh

Child of Bethlehem

Child of Bethlehem,
when your fingers
wrap themselves
round one of ours,
and your eyes
focus on our face,
you look for love in us:
love for friends,
for God and strangers,
love for the earth,
love for enemies,
love that says
Yes to life.

Ruth Burgess

Mary and Joseph at Capstone Farm

This story sets the birth of Jesus at Capstone Farm in Kent, where my great-grandfather and grandfather had been farm bailiff and then my father farm manager.

This I remember:

Topsy being milked, the warmth of the stable filled with space and sunlight, her rich and soft and golden-brown coat, the swish, swish, swish of milk into the bucket, the closeness of man and beast, his head pressed into her side.

Topsy was the Jersey cow we had for my grandmother, who couldn't abide 'milkman's muck'.

Also in the stable was Dapple, the last of the shire horses my father worked, huge, but gentle and friendly, to be treated with care and respect. He was freely and willingly given the time he needed and deserved for grooming and feeding, clearing and cleaning his stable, putting down fresh bedding and filling his manger with straw and hay that smelt of sunshine and the joy and laughter of harvest.

That winter's night, after we children had gone to bed, Dad had made two homeless travellers comfortable. There was hay and straw, a roof over their heads and a door to shut out the night. There was running water in the tap outside and an oil lamp for light. They were glad to stop and rest and share the space with Topsy and Dapple. Dad was able to let them have a stall to themselves.

He walked across the farmyard and along our garden and in the back door. Mum had just made a pot of tea. He told her about the pregnant woman, near her time, and about her husband. His last words before he went to bed were 'not to interfere': we could contact social services in the morning. They would be all right till then.

When it was quiet upstairs Mum rang down to Gran at the farmhouse. They plotted to wait until Dad was asleep when Mum would creep out and go down to Gran. Meanwhile, Gran would get blankets and pillows airing by the range and the kettle would be on with a tray ready with cups, saucers and a plate of homemade cake.

Finally Mum crept out of our house into the quiet stillness of the night. She hurried down the road, past the farmyard, in at the garden gate and into the back door of the farmhouse. Between them they carried blankets, pillows and a tray of tea through the side gate and into the side yard. As they got nearer to the stable they could hear that labour had started.

The man was managing pretty well, but happy to let them take over and glad of the hot tea and cake. Gran went back for hot water and clean towels. In spite of being fastidious and easily embarrassed my mother set to, made the woman as comfortable as she could and kept watch with her through her labour. Finally, in the early hours of the morning, the baby boy was born. They wrapped him in a towel and gave him to his mother to hold while they waited for the placenta to be born. Then they placed him in the hay-filled manger while they tidied up his mother and left her to sleep.

By now it was morning and Mum came back home, took my father his early morning cup of tea and told him what they'd done. She woke us children and after breakfast took us to see the baby in the stable.

He was so tiny, with beautiful little fingers and perfect pink nails. He looked at me with those solemn, old-young eyes newborn babies have. He grasped my finger and I loved him. I wanted to look after him, protect him, share my secrets with him, help him to learn and grow and to be his friend.

Pamela Whyman

Yusuf was bored

Yusuf was bored and everyone was busy. He was only eight so he wasn't allowed to wander past the end of his street, especially not this week with all the travellers and people in the town.

It wasn't fair no one had time for him and most people pushed by without even noticing he was there! It wasn't fair he was the youngest and all his brothers and sisters were either old enough to help at the inn or at least allowed to play with their friends without having to 'stay close'.

They called him a baby, but he was eight – he knew his way around. It was silly and he was bored, fed up – and it wasn't fair!

Yusuf sat on the rock at the end of his street. It was a big rock, too big to be moved when they were building the inn. It was so big that all the carts and people had to go round it, but it had a flat top and at least it was good for sitting.

So Yusuf, bored and hard done by, watched the people pass. There were some Roman soldiers in their leather armour with their hard faces and big spears. There were rich people in fine clothes, some even dressed in purple. There were travellers on donkeys, horses and even big camels from the east.

There was dust and smells. The smell of bread, with sesame seeds sprinkled on top, baked in the local ovens, the smell of the camels, and of the heavy perfumes of the rich travellers, and of the olive oil and spices from the inn's kitchen.

Yusuf watched and noticed a lot – being the youngest, and having busy parents who ran the inn, and not being allowed to wander past the end of the street marked by the big rock on which he sat.

People are interesting, even when you were bored, thought Yusuf, and he tried to guess where the people came from and what they did.

Coming up the hill to the inn he saw a donkey with two people beside it: a tall man and a young woman, who looked as if she was not feeling very well.

They struggled while all the busy people pushed past. Yusuf was so busy watching them, he did not notice a camel laden with spices coming towards his rock, and a cart full of hay coming in the other direction. And he did not have time to avoid the big sack falling from the camel's back and knocking him into the road, and no one noticed him.

The next thing Yusuf saw and heard was a gentle hand wiping the dirt from his face and a kind voice asking him if he was all right. When he looked up, there was the couple with the donkey who had been finding their journey hard. While everybody else had been rushing past, they had seen his fall and had come to help. The man lifted him up in his strong arms and the young woman asked him where he lived.

The couple gently placed him on the donkey and they walked the few yards to the inn.

Yusuf's parents were glad to see that he was OK and grateful to the couple for saving him.

They sat them down and gave them some sweet-smelling lamb stew and some wine, but Yusuf's mother was concerned about the woman: she had seen the pain in her face and realised that she was going to have a baby very soon.

The inn was full, so Yusuf's mother sent his big brother Elias to ask the other innkeepers if they had any rooms.

Everybody told him the same thing – they were full and could not help.

'Mum,' said Yusuf, 'when Elias and his friends are helping with the olive harvest you often let them stay in the stable overnight, and they say it's fun, and that the animals make it warm.'

His mother smiled. 'Go to the stable and get clean straw, Yusuf, and tell Miriam to get some hot water and some clean sheets.'

The man, who was also called Yusuf, lifted his wife, Mary, and carried her to the stable.

It was not long before the baby was born, and when he cried for the first time everyone was very happy.

The family were a little embarrassed that the kind couple were where they were but they did everything they could to make them welcome and comfortable, for they were special people and had saved Yusuf.

Yusuf could not drag himself away, and even when his mother had sent him to bed he sneaked out and tiptoed to the stable. He was really surprised when he saw lots of local shepherds gathered around. This baby is different, he thought, and just then, between the wooden slats of the stable door, Yusuf's eyes met the eyes of the baby and Yusuf smiled and the baby seemed to smile back.

Yusuf looked up into the clear night sky and amidst all the wonderful stars he saw one glow more brightly over the stable.

For some reason the baby's birth caused a bit of a stir, and for years later people talked about the inn in Bethlehem beside the big rock.

Yusuf never forgot that night and for all of his life he remembered the kindness of that day and the wonder of the night.

Mary and the man who was also called Yusuf named their baby Jesus, and many other stories were written about him. He was special and grew up to be as kind as anyone could be.

Yusuf did not know how special Jesus would be, or anything about his parents when he met them, but kindness was shared and lives changed.

Tonight and every night, open your hearts and hands to help the people who come your way, for a good deed is always a gift and everyone is special to God.

Stuart Fulton

Lord Jesus, hear our prayer

Jesus, whose mother was Mary:
we pray for families of all shapes and sizes
all over the world.
Lord Jesus,
Hear our prayer.

Jesus, cradled in a manger,
we pray for those who have no home,
and for those who have left behind all they know.
Lord Jesus,
Hear our prayer.

Jesus, sharing the stable with the animals,
we pray that we might treat the animals and plants
which share our world with kindness and respect.
Lord Jesus,
Hear our prayer.

Jesus, worshipped by shepherds and kings,
we pray for all kinds of people
all over the world.
Lord Jesus,
Hear our prayer.

Jesus, our Emmanuel,
we pray for those people who especially need
to know God is with them this Christmastime.
Lord Jesus,
Hear our prayer.

S Anne Lawson

Earth-dwelling God

Earth-dwelling God,
willing to be made small and vulnerable,
choosing to live with the ordinary people on earth,
we come before you in wide-eyed wonder.

We join in with the stars as they sing for joy;
our hearts echo the music of angels
which filled the skies on the night of your birth.

With outrageous humility
you share our humanity;
you are our God made flesh,
revealed among us for all to see.
And it takes our breath away.

As we gather again
to celebrate your birth
and proclaim your love,
may your peace fill our world
and joy transcend all fear.

And may we ever find you
at one with your people,
sharing our pain,
making us whole.
Amen

Louise Gough

Oh, that we were there

(Tune: 'Masters in the hall', French traditional)

Oh, that we were there, standing 'neath the star,
sent there by the angels, shepherds from afar.

Chorus: Noel nouvelet, O Noel nouvelet,*
home for now his mother's arms and
a manger full of hay;
Noel nouvelet, O Noel nouvelet.
Come the end of Advent toil,
come the dawn of Christmas day.

Oh, that we were there, brought out by a star,
caravan of strangers, magi from afar:

Chorus

Oh, that we were there, longing to give birth.
God to us has spoken, glory comes to earth:

Chorus

Nudging human hearts, the poor will hear his call;
sent there by each other, come we to his stall:

Chorus

Bring the gift we own: gold and incense, myrrh;
share the gifts He's grown, offer who we are:

Chorus

da Noust

* Sung: 'No-el nou-vel-lay'

The Angel Tam

Wander into the church dressed like a fairy. Change town names and dialect to your own locality.

I am the Angel Tam.

I am meant to be a messenger from God.

I am supposed to inspire awe and terror into the hearts of men and women and wee weans that look at me.

But because of the credit crunch this year, all they could give me to wear was this leftover fairy costume from last year's Christmas panto!

Och, it's no easy being a messenger of God today.

I mean we turn up in all sorts of costumes, you know.

We don't often appear today with wee angel wings and halos round our heids!

Sometimes we appear in jeans and T-shirts.

Sometimes we turn up dressed like neds in tracksuits and bunnets, or in the latest designer gear wi' a great big cheque book in our hands tae help some worthy cause.

Sometimes ye'll see us dressed up in black, and the halo has slipped around our necks tae look like a dog collar.

Sometimes in the schools we come dressed in trendy ties tae impress the weans, and they just think we're a bunch of heidbangers, talking about things they dinnae understand or believe in.

You know, it's no wonder today that folk dinnae understand our message.

A lang time ago, God said me, 'Haw, Tam, I've got a wee job for ye.'

(My name is no really Tam, it's Gabriel, but everybody just thought I was a big lassie, so ah changed it tae Tam so that it wid be mair manly like.)

God said: 'Go unto earth to a virgin espoused to a man whose name is Joseph, of the house of David, and the virgin's name is Mary.'

Ah said: 'Haw, God, you gonnae talk in a way that I can un'erstaun? I mean what does "espoused to a man whose name is Joseph" mean?'

God gave me one of his looks and then said. 'Tam, just go and tell Mary and Joseph they are going to have a baby. To be "espoused" means they are going to get married.'

Well, I went in search of Mary and Joseph all over the world. I had a quick look in Dunipace but couldnae find any wise men there, and I had great difficulty finding a virgin in Falkirk; but eventually I met Mary and Joseph in a wee place called Nazareth, which was really a bit like Denny today!

Poor Mary nearly died when I appeared out of nowhere and said: 'Mary doll, I have some good news and bad news for you. The good news is that you're going to have a wedding soon, but the bad news is, it will no be quite a white wedding … and by the way, you are gonnae hae a wee boy soon and ye huv tae call him Jesus.'

Poor Mary was fair flabergas … fluberg … was fair shattered wi' the news. She tried tae tell me that she was as pure as the driven snow and that no man had so much as kissed her, and how dare I come and cast aspersions towards her womanhood.

Ye ken, she was a right fiery wee wuman was Mary.

I said, 'Mary, … doll, this is nae ordinary baby you are going tae huv, it's a special baby. God himself is gonnae gie ye a son, and I'll square everything with Joseph fur ye.'

The poor lassie burst out greeting, but I reassured her that she would be blessed amongst all woman and highly favoured, and that seemed to do the trick.

Joseph on the other hand wisnae so easy tae convince. He gave me a whole list o' suspects who he said had fancied Mary, and he wis wantin' tae dump her when I telt him aboot the baby.

But in the end I talked them roon, and they set off to Bethlehem fur the census that King Herod had ordered.

By the time thae got tae Bethlehem where a' Joseph's relatives were fae, the place was packed. Mary was about tae drap her son at ony time, and Joseph had forgot to book in advance in the Christmas rush. They ended up in a stable fur the night, sleeping wae the cows and sheep but Mary was that tired she didnae care any longer.

And then it happened.

Wee Jesus was born, in the stable that night.

And afore ye knew it, there were shepherds and wise men, and kings and folk queuing up at the door tae get a look at this wee baby, who God said had come tae be the Saviour o' the world.

And dae ye ken, the world has been a different kind a place ever since, for God himself came intae the world tae show us how we could live in a way that pleased him, ourselves and everybody round aboot us.

Ah well, I could be here all night telling ye tales of Angel Tam, but I think I better go and get changed intae some ither clothes.

Don't be feart! I'll no' get changed afore ye!

John Murning, Spill the Beans

Are you ready?
A Christmas Eve play

As the minister speaks, the angel (dressed in wings and an apron and carrying a duster) begins to make his/her way down the central aisle, dusting, cleaning ...

Minister: *(to congregation)* It's almost time, you know. Are you ready? Well, we here at the Cathedral *(church ...)* definitely are. The Advent candles are lit, the tree is up, the Christingle bags are out, and in a minute we'll all be putting them together. I've delivered my Christmas cards and – *(notices the angel and stops speaking)* ...

Angel: *(The angel notices that the talking has stopped and looks up.)* Sorry, I didn't mean to disturb you – just checking that everything's ready.

Minister: I can assure you – everything's ready for Christmas. Who are you anyway?

Angel: *(points to wings)* I thought that was kind of obvious: I'm an angel.

Minister: But what are you doing here? It's Christmas Eve – shouldn't you be away somewhere singing or delivering a message – you know, angel stuff?

Angel: Well, I am delivering a message. The message is YOU'RE NOT AS READY AS YOU THINK YOU ARE.

Minister: What are you talking about? Look at the tree, the Advent candles – all these people. We're ready.

Angel: What about the baby?

Minister: What do you mean, the baby?

Angel: The baby that's going to be born tonight.

Minister: But he's not really being born ... it's just a celebration.

Angel: If you say so ... But, I am the angel *(turns to go)*.

Minister:	W … Wait a minute. Not that I believe you, but just supposing … what would we need, for a baby?
Angel:	A baby needs to be warm. The most important thing a new baby needs – anybody needs – is to know they're wanted and welcome.
Minister:	A blanket would keep the baby warm and make him, or her, feel secure.
Angel:	Good idea. Arms are good too. Sometimes hugs can be as good as a blanket. Remember that.
Minister:	Ahh … OK, anyway, I don't think we have anything like that around here.
Angel:	Are you sure? Maybe some of these children would look under the pews. There might be something unexpected. It is Christmas Eve. Go on – have a look … Any luck? If you've found a blanket, bring it up and place it in the manger. *(A child brings the blanket up.)*
Minister:	I can't imagine where that came from.
Angel:	Welcomes come from the most unexpected places – especially on Christmas Eve.
Minister:	What else do we need, just in case?
Angel:	Another thing that babies want – everybody wants – is a little light in dark places. It's comforting and makes them feel safe.
Minister:	We don't have that either. We've got the Cathedral lights, but those go out when we leave.
Angel:	I think I saw a lantern at the back of the Cathedral – in one of the pews. Could the person sitting next to it bring it up here, or give it to someone nearby to bring it? … *(The light is brought forward.)* There. That's better.
Minister:	Well, I have to admit – it is looking a lot cosier up here now. I suppose the only thing left is food. The baby will need something to eat.

Angel:	His mum can sort that out, but she and the dad will probably be starving. What about something for them?
Minister:	I don't think there's any food in the Cathedral.
Angel:	You keep forgetting that it's Christmas Eve and unexpected things happen tonight. I think there might be something in the pulpit.
Minister:	Does someone want to go up and see? *(A bag of food, goodies is brought forward.)* OK, I think we're ready now – ready for Jesus to be born.
Angel:	Who said I was talking about Jesus?
Minister:	But you said –
Angel:	I said, 'Are you ready for the baby that's going to be born tonight?' And there will be many babies born tonight. They all need a welcome, and warmth, a little light for their journey and a fair share of food. When Jesus was grown up he told us to always remember that he can be found in the little ones, the unlikely ones, the unexpected one – so be ready.
Minister:	*(disappointedly)* So, he's not really being born … it's just a celebration?
Angel:	If you say so … But, I am the angel. *(The angel turns and goes.)*

Sally Foster-Fulton

God who loves to be with us

God who loves to be with us,
when you were born
you were born into a community.

Gather us as your community tonight.

A community of young and old,
a community of those with status and influence and those with none,
a community of different genders and races,
a community that includes people and animals and the whole of creation.

Gather us as a community that meets in joy:
a community that has heard the angels' song of peace and goodwill,
a community that has seen a star in the sky
and has followed it.

God who loves to be with us,
gather us into your community tonight;
help us to welcome you,
and to welcome each other
in kindness and caring love. Amen

Margery Toller

A crib prayer

Lord, we bring our candles to your crib.

We bring our songs to your crib,
we bring our praise to your crib,
we bring our lives to your crib.
Bless this crib as it tells the story of Christmas for us.

Bless your family gathered here,
as we sing the songs of Christmas
and worship you tonight.

Judy Dinnen

Christmas Eve tonight

When the angels had left them and gone into heaven, the shepherds said to one another, 'Let us go now to Bethlehem and see this thing that has taken place, which the Lord has made known to us.' So they went with haste and found Mary and Joseph, and the child lying in the manger. (Luke 2:15–16)

Every year when the all too familiar story from Luke is read on Christmas Eve on TV, the angel who speaks to the shepherds usually does so with a voice like that of actor James Earl Jones. And the choir? Well, it has to be the Mormon Tabernacle Choir, right? Or something like that.

But this year, finally, I saw and heard the choir as it must have really been on that night in Bethlehem. Residents of the care centre where Teddy my son lives marched in with heads held high, wearing robes that had apparently been found stuffed in a closet somewhere, music folders clutched nervously in their hands. Their voices did not meld perfectly, they tended to wander around trying to find the notes, their words were not clearly enunciated or projected …

But when they started to sing 'Silent night' – the soloist's voice beginning with a tremble and then growing in confidence – that was the moment when Mr Jones' voice left my mind, and that choir which has recorded so many albums sat down with me to listen. For this was the sound the shepherds heard on the hillside – that sent them running down to Bethlehem to find this joy. These were the voices that shattered the complacency of history and forever transformed the hopes of humanity. After all, who better than the most vulnerable to announce that God has chosen to set aside glory and become weak; who better than those the world discounts to tell us of the One who has come to embrace all with God's love; who better than our broken children to sing to us of the Child who will make us – each and every one of us – whole? …

This is the choir, these are the voices I will hear from now on on Christmas Eve, hoping that, when eternity comes, they might let me sing with them.

Thom M Shuman

Watchnight

He walked alone on Christmas Eve

A meditation for anyone who has gone out late on the night before Christmas for a Communion service and wondered whether it was worth it.

He heaved on his boots and opened the door. The air was cold outside and flowed over his face with icy contempt.

How many more times? he thought. How many times had it been so far? More than he could tell.

And it was always the same.

They said, 'You'll be there first, won't you? So can you prepare what's needed? We'll be along later. You don't mind, do you?'

Would it matter if I did, he would wonder. But he didn't really mind. It was just what had come to be expected. It was part of his work.

But tonight the air seemed colder, the boots heavier and his bag cut into his shoulder.

He closed the gate and turned down the hill until he came to the high street. There was no one in sight. This was the part he really liked. The cars were parked, already catching their first sheen of frost. There was light everywhere.

The shop lights shone out across the street, the council lights had already been shut down (austerity, bah!), Christmas tree lights still twinkled on the sides of the houses, and he could take his time.

He would not meet anyone.

He walked slowly, sometimes stopping to gaze into the shops. Some still advertised their seasonal wares but now they seemed past it, rather forlorn – no more shopping days till Xmas. Some had got their New Year's bargains in place, already reaching out with the fiendish grip of commercial entrapment.

As he walked on he could hear the sound of laughter from inside the cottages. Some had left their curtains drawn and he could look in on festive lamps and parcels ready for the morning. He did not stop. He felt like a stranger invited to gaze in but not enter.

He shook himself. This was no way to do his job on Christmas Eve.

'Get a grip, man, you know you are always like this. Stop feeling sorry for yourself.'

He left the street behind and began to climb the lane toward the church. It stood solid and still. Its light-toned stone reflected the moonlight that had suddenly appeared.

'This will get them out – it all looks just like the Xmas cards they send each other. All we need now is light snow – not too much or it will lie.'

He chided his bleak and frosty cynicism.

He turned the key of the lock and the heavy door swung open. A solitary candle was alight on the table. Slowly, with care and unhurried mind now, he began the preparation.

The gentle moving of cloth and plate, cup and book; familiar gestures of age-old reverence stilled his mind and let in his faith. When all was done at the table he turned toward the still-empty church.

'We'll be along later. You don't mind, do you?'

But he knew he was not alone. He never had been. There were no empty seats in the church. They awaited their customers. Beyond the gaze of human eye in the light-shaped shadows of the old building there was a great company of previous occupants.

The few that night who would worship did so among a numberless company called by the Grace of God, who had plodded along the same high street and climbed the same lane on a journey begun many miles and years before on a track to the City of David.

And for a brief moment the tired minister with numb feet, aching shoulders and lonely faith could look out over the still sanctuary and see faces, real faces. The faces of those he had known there and beyond the tiny village who had walked with him and kept the faith down through the years.

He had not walked alone on Christmas Eve.

John Rackley

All this night

Words & music by Roddy Cowie

All this night, God's world lies waiting, sensing more than humans know: high on lonely winter hillsides sheep look up to stars aglow. Silence deepens, Heaven trembles, music ripples on the wind: light and glory split the sky, and

Words and music © Roddy Cowie

All this night, God's world lies waiting,
sensing more than humans know:
high on lonely winter hillsides
sheep look up to stars aglow.
Silence deepens, Heaven trembles,
music ripples on the wind:
light and glory split the sky,
and song floods ears and hearts and minds.

Glory be to God the Father,
source and Lord of all that is:
peace to those his mercy blesses,
joy to those he greets as his.
Wonder courses through creation,
knowing what his hand has done:
passing through the gate of flesh
to shine on earth as God the Son.

Glory breaks on winter hillsides,
sweeping through the town below,
breaking chains of time and space
to set us singing as we go.
Glory, sing the heights of Heaven,
Glory, sings the human heart:
God has bound himself to us
in bonds no force or fire can part.

Roddy Cowie

The bothy

Every room will be blazing with
light,
so I will have no trouble
finding the place
when I arrive, or so I
imagine:
the table covered in fine
lace,
heirloom china
and mirrored silver at each
place
with the feast's aroma
drifting in from the kitchen;
my feather bed will manger
my weary body while
silk sheets swaddle me to sleep
after a relaxing soak
in the jet-streamed tub.

But
what if it is
just a box built out of
river rocks,
the door wind-weathered
and water-buckled,
refusing to stay shut
as if expecting more folk;
a rough-hewn shelf
in one of the corners
holds a clay pitcher brimming
with cool clear water,
a hand-drawn map to the spring
next to it;
wood has been laid
in the fireplace,

ready to be brought to
life;
a stone shelf is all that keeps
one's body from the ground,
just wide and long enough
for a rough blanket,
a candle and matches
where the pillow would be;
and there's a shovel
by the door for taking care
of the necessaries;

it seemed perfect for
you
when you arrived,
didn't it?

Thom M Shuman

Christmas came simply

Christmas
came simply:
a pregnant woman
a worried father
a night birth
a healthy child.

Just God
unwrapped,
vulnerable,
lying in a manger,
living in our world.

Ruth Burgess

It was dark

For two voices

It was dark,
really dark,
like completely dark,
totally dark,
couldn't see your hand in front of your face dark,
so it was really, really dark.

Next minute there was tons of light,
like, mega-light,
bright like you've never experienced before,
needing sunglasses light,
light that burned into your eyes
and left after-images.

And it was caused by angels,
real angels,
dressed in white and wearing halos angels,
wings that beat with gold flashes angels,
angels that just appeared in one instant out of the darkness
and exploded in waves across the sky.
But they weren't silent angels.
Oh no, they sang like Metallica angels,
big voices that roared as they sang angels,
a big noisy word that filled the sky with noise angels,
a great big word sung together angels –
Alleluia.

The shepherds, they just stood there,
like totally still shepherds,
statue-like shepherds,
with jaws open shepherds,
catching flies shepherds,
shepherds who had never seen anything like it before.

Suddenly the song changed,
like totally changed,
the angel song morphed into an angel shout:
voices rising to a new level angel shout,
all joining in together angel shout
like a complete choral reading.

The song of 'Alleluia' became the shout of 'peace',
for the entire earth peace,
to completely everyone peace,
total peace,
to the whole world peace,
peace takes over peace.

'Jesus is born,' they shouted,
like straight out they shouted:
'Jesus is born, go and see him!'
'Too right! Let's go to Bethlehem right now
and see this thing that has happened,' the shepherds shouted.
And as they shouted off they went.

Right then, to the stable,
to that Bethlehem round the back of the inn stable,
in a world that was very unstable,
and saw there the one thing that brought stay-ability,
alive in a manger.
So let us stay close, and let him stay in us.

Roddy Hamilton, Spill the Beans

In the darkness

In the darkness
we wait for Christmas:
some of us are happy,
some of us are sad.

In the darkness
we wait for Christmas:
some of us are believers,
some of us are unsure.

In the darkness
we wait for Christmas:
some of us have houses full of presents,
some of us are struggling to survive.

In the darkness
we wait for Christmas:
we cannot see each other's faces,
we do not know each other's pains and joys.

In the darkness
we wait for Christmas:
we wait for a baby
who is about to be born.

In the darkness
we wait for Christmas:
we wait and we wonder,
we hope for love.

In the darkness
we wait for Christmas:
we wait for Jesus
to bring light to our world.

In the darkness
we wait for Christmas
and God waits with us.
God is here in this place.

In the darkness
we wait for Christmas:
and we hear the story
that tells of God's love.

In the darkness
the choice is ours.
Will we stay in the darkness
or come to the light?

Ruth Burgess, Spill the Beans

A Christmas blessing

May the news of the angels
fill your life and your heart with great joy.

May the star that guided the wise
lead you to the truth of understanding.

May the witness of the shepherds
affirm in you the message of the Gospel.

May the sound of the incarnate Word
bring you peace and hope.

May the presence of the sacred baby
remind you of your own holiness.

And
may this Christmas
gift you
bless you
comfort you
inspire you,
as you journey into another year.
Amen

Peter Siney

A prayer for others

We pray for all
who watch and wait this night:
those who watch for death,
those who wait for birth.

We pray especially for those who watch and wait alone
in fear or with longing,
where circumstances are far from ideal
and conditions far from sanitary,
for all those hidden away lest their
predicament should taint the revelry of others.

We pray for all who are far from home,
especially those forced to flee their home
because of injustice and oppression,
those rendered homeless by poverty or violence.

May the piercing cry of a child
in the darkness
be a symbol of hope for a world
weary with suffering.

May the soft footfall of shepherds
replace the ominous march
of soldiers' boots.
And, however unlikely it might seem,
may peace gain a foothold tonight
as God's people rediscover hope
in hidden places and hear angel song
above the noise of war.

May we hold our collective breath
and find light creeping in
to nudge the darkness
of the world into submission,
as love pushes at the boundaries
making change a possibility.

And so may the stable
become a sign of stability.
May the star become the sign of potential.
And may the cradle be the sign of promise for all the world.
Amen

Liz Crumlish, Spill the Beans

Hope came

Hope came,
curling up in bed
next to the little
girl
who cries herself
to sleep each night,
as her parents
argue in the
next room;

grace came,
thumbing through the old
magazines
while sitting silently
in the chair next
to the hospital
bed,
so when the old
man
awoke, he
would see a familiar
face;

love came,
cracking her back
as she stretched arms
to the ceiling,

trying to work out
the kinks
from cooking all
night
for the families
sound asleep in
the community centre's
hall;

peace came,
taking weapons out
of our hands, so
we could build
bridges
and tear down
walls;

you came …
… you
came!

Just as you
promised.

Thom M Shuman

Light, to crumple up the darkness

This Christmas
I wish for you,
light,
to crumple up the darkness.

This Christmas
I wish for you,
love,
to pull us closer to one another.

This Christmas
I wish for you,
peace,
of which the angels sang.

This Christmas
I wish for you,
starlight,
to follow you on your way home.

This Christmas
I wish for you,
God's promise,
to keep hope alive for you.

This Christmas
I wish for you,
God,
newly born and in the flesh.

This Christmas
I wish for you,
Jesus Christ,
born this night,
light of the world.

Roddy Hamilton, Spill the Beans

Christmas Day

God in a manger

God in a manger,
God of surprises,
help us to unwrap
your present to us
this Christmas:
show us how to celebrate
your birth simply,
with justice
and with holy joy. Amen

Ruth Burgess

No and yes

The innkeeper was used to saying 'No'. He'd been saying 'No' all night.

'No, you can't get a room here tonight.'

'No, you can't have more towels.'

'No, you can't get another pudding.'

'No, you can't invite your mother-in-law and her whole family to share your room.'

'No, no, no, no, NO!'

It had made him very grumpy. In fact he was always grumpy. And then the doorbell went once more …

'Oh no,' he said. 'Do they *not* know there is no more room?'

He swung open the door and was about to launch into his usual spiel about there being no room, when he hesitated and stuttered.

He was aware he was trying to say 'No' because he was so used to saying 'No' but this man looked so concerned and this woman was clearly about to have a baby, and his lips were moving in another direction and instead of 'No' he found himself saying 'Yes' and it surprised him how good that felt.

Mary and Joseph, who were the ones standing at the door, looked at each other, and then at the innkeeper and said, 'But we haven't asked you anything.'

The innkeeper just said, 'Yes.'

'So you have room?' asked Joseph.

'Yes,' said the innkeeper, who was feeling particularly good now.

'For two of us and perhaps a baby?'

'Yes,' said the innkeeper and a smile grew round his face.

'In here?' questioned Joseph. 'Or round the back?'

'Yes,' said the innkeeper; he was positively beaming.

'Which?' asked Joseph.

'Sorry,' said the innkeeper coming out of his daze, 'round the back.'

So he took them to a stable where it was warm, though the innkeeper's smile was even warmer. And having let Mary and Joseph in, he stood by the door of the stable while Jesus was born, guarding it.

Later, as a bundle of shepherds arrived, asking to see the new baby, the innkeeper found himself saying only one thing: 'Yes. Come in. There is room. There is always room.'

And such has been the way of all those caught up in the Christmas story: Mary, shepherds, Joseph, travellers, and now the innkeeper.

The answer to Christmas is 'Yes', and it changes everything.

Roddy Hamilton, Spill the Beans

In memoriam

Our Christmas bird this year was not the lordly turkey,
with its flotilla of potatoes round it, sailing the rippling grease;
nor yet the robin hopping its way about the frosted cherry tree:
it was a gull, cold at the road's edge, as the night began to freeze.

Huddled there, puffier than gulls look in the sky, greyer,
and so still it might have been a toy discarded by the childish air,
tossed into a driveway: but the head shifted a fraction here and there
so listless that it seemed the overwhelming impulse was despair.

As if its gull love had been swept away from it by a marauding younger gull;
or it had read an aerobatic turn a millimetre wrong, and smashed its skull
into the ugly glitter of a window pane; or it had flown beside the moon
  when it was full
and understood that it could never be so high, or white, or wonderful.

We brought it in, not thinking it would live, but to forestall the certainty
that if we left it to the cats and frost, they would ensure it died.
It found the energy to eat a little bread, and we were hopeful for a while;
but in the night it fluttered piteously, and had no strength to cry.

I knew it then, and in the morning it was lying with its wings outspread,
all of its struggles over, but the black piercing eyes still open wide.
We took it to the river, and we spilled its body on the riverside,
trusting the river water to absorb its pain as the rain swelled the tide.

Let this be understood as a memorial
left by a human being to a broken gull;
not thinking that I understood at all,
without a valid word to say:
but on a Christmas day,
needing a gift for the departed life, however small.

Roddy Cowie

Aren't primary-school Nativity plays embarrassing?

Aren't primary-school Nativity plays embarrassing?
Tea-towelled and dressing-gowned children shuffle onto the stage,
trying to see their parents,
guided and prompted by motherly teachers and assistants.
Wobbly singing, wooden recitations.

Saint Luke doesn't actually mention a stable,
or an innkeeper.
Saint Matthew doesn't tell us how many wise men came.
They probably weren't kings;
they came months after the birth.
And I've never seen a Nativity play that included a child-murdering,
paranoid psychopath.
They are all cute fairy stories.

But I've just seen one that was different –
moving, sincere, touching, full of spiritual meaning.
My granddaughter was a sheep.

Brian Ford

The song of the angels

May the song of the angels,
the joy of the shepherds,
the wonder of the wise men,
and the peace of the newborn king
fill our hearts and homes
this Christmastime and always.
Amen

Simon Taylor

The Lord of life

Words: Colin and Carol Dixon. Music: Colin Dixon

Words and music © Colin and Carol Dixon

Christmas Day 203

*Chorus: Jesus was born here on our earth
to show us God with a human face.
Jesus came to share our birth,
bringing light to the human race.*

The Lord of heav'n, he comes to us,
a simple babe in a stable born,
the Lord of love, he lives in us,
our Saviour God, this Christmas morn.

Chorus

The Lord of Life, Emmanuel,
God with us as a lowly king,
the Prince of Peace, the mighty God,
Christ is born, his praises sing:

Chorus (and repeat chorus)

Words: Colin and Carol Dixon. Music: Colin Dixon

We believe in Christmas

We believe in Christmas.
We believe that the words of the prophet that speak of justice
to the oppressed
and care for the widow are God's Word that sets the world free.
For love came down at Christmas.
We believe in Christmas.

We believe in Christmas.
We believe that the light of the world that crushes all darkness
and exposes all lies
is God's light that shines through every darkness.
For love came down at Christmas.
We believe in Christmas.

We believe in Christmas.
We believe that the song of the angels that celebrates peace on earth
and to all people on the earth
is God's peace that the world cannot find but Jesus can offer.
For love came down at Christmas.
We believe in Christmas.

We believe in Christmas
We believe that Mary's poem Magnificat, where God turns everything upside down,
where the poor are lifted up and the powerful are brought down,
is God's poem that changes the balance of the world.
For love came down at Christmas.
We believe in Christmas.

We believe in Christmas.
We believe the Word becomes flesh,
the promise is fulfilled,
the light breaks through,
the oppressed are set free,
the lowly are lifted up
and the baby cries.
For love came down at Christmas.
We believe in Christmas.

Roddy Hamilton, Spill the Beans

Bidding prayers

In the beginning – you were.
In this moment – you are.
You are strength and weakness.
You are light and glory.
You are God and you welcome us:
you listen for our prayers …

We pray today for peace, peace in Bethlehem, peace in the dark places of our world. We pray for leaders and negotiators, for peacemakers and peacekeepers, for fighters and prisoners, for all who are caught up in conflict, violence and fear.
We pray for peace with integrity and with justice …
God, in your mercy,
Hear our prayer.

We pray for children everywhere, for the newly born, for those growing up among us, for those growing up in places where there is poverty and danger. We pray that they may be loved and welcomed and that they may know smiles and hope …
God, in your mercy,
Hear our prayer.

We pray for all who sit and eat with us today. We thank you for our families, for our friends, for those who love us, for those who share our laughter and pain. We pray for those who, by choice or by circumstance, eat alone. And we pray for justice for those who are hungry …
God, in your mercy,
Hear our prayer.

We pray for all who are sick and for those who care for them and pray for them. We pray for those who have died, for those we miss at our table. Tell them how much we love them, we miss them, we carry their stories in our lives …
God, in your mercy,
Hear our prayer.

We pray for ourselves, for our needs, our concerns,
our hopes and our dreams …
God, in your mercy,
Hear our prayer.

Bright loving God, Emmanuel, God-with-us,
help us to recognise you today
and to welcome you into our lives
in wonder, in truth and in holy joy.
Amen

Ruth Burgess

A Christmas Day blessing

Emmanuel,
God-with-us,
bless us and caress us
this Christmas day
and all the days of our lives. Amen

Ruth Burgess

Look, Lord, said the angels
(Tune: 'Away in a manger')

'Look, Lord,' said the angels,
'they've had a fair chance
your will to obey and
your cause to advance –
but humans are fickle;
they go as they please:
so close down the shutters
and cancel their lease.'

But God said, 'I've promised
to stay at their side
in faithful commitment
as bridegroom with bride.
The struggle with evil
in heaven begun
must get earthly focus:
I'll come in my Son.'

No heavenly pillow
supports the wee head;
no hygiene, no midwifely
care for blood shed.
A mark of the Kingdom,
of world's hope increased,
is God's son is classed
with the lowest and least.

We hail Mary's vision
of change Jesus led:
the powerful brought low
and the hungry well-fed.
The Kingdom's brought nearer
when we follow God's way;
with birth in a stable
God has come here to stay.

Ian M Fraser

The Christmas story

Luke and Matthew
(For two voices)

> *Matthew the storyteller wears a bright coat/long bright scarf. Luke the storyteller carries a shepherd's crook and/or carries a toy sheep.*

A long time ago a man called Luke wrote down some stories about Jesus.

While Luke was writing his book about Jesus another man called Matthew was writing a book about Jesus too.

Luke listened to lots of stories that people remembered about Jesus and he also looked at a book that a man called Mark had written about Jesus' life.

Matthew looked at Mark's book too and he asked lots of people to tell him what they remembered about what Jesus talked about and how Jesus lived.

Luke wrote down some stories about when Jesus was born, and we're going to listen to one of his stories in a minute.

Matthew wrote down some stories about Jesus as a baby too. They were different stories to the ones Luke told – because he'd heard the stories from different people. We'll hear one of his stories too.

Once, said Luke, when Augustus was the Roman Emperor, he ordered a census to be taken. He wanted a count to be made of all the people who lived in the Roman Empire. This meant that people had to travel to the places where their families came from, to be counted.

Once, said Matthew, when Herod was the king of Judea, there were some wise men who lived in an eastern country. They spent time together at night looking at the stars. They thought that the movement of the stars in the sky could tell them what was happening in the world.

There was a man called Joseph, wrote Luke, who lived in Nazareth, but his family came from Bethlehem, which was 50 miles away. So Joseph had to go to Bethlehem on a certain day to be counted. Joseph was married, and his wife, who was called Mary, was expecting a baby. Mary had to go with Joseph to Bethlehem. It was going to be a long journey.

One day, wrote Matthew, a new star appeared in the sky. The wise men were very excited. The star began to move across the skies and the men decided that they would go and follow the star and see where it led them. What an adventure!

When Mary and Joseph got to Bethlehem they tried to find somewhere to stay. Lots of people's families came from Bethlehem and the town was very busy. It was nearly time for Mary's baby to be born. Joseph searched the town for somewhere to stay. At last he found an innkeeper who told him that they could stay in the stable at the back of the inn. They were exhausted, but very glad that they had found somewhere to rest.

Before the wise men set off they talked about what this new star meant. They decided that it meant that a new king, an important king, had been born. They decided to take some presents for the new king with them. They travelled, following the star, for many days. The star seemed to be leading them towards Jerusalem, so they thought that they had better call in at the palace and ask King Herod what he knew about the new king.

In the stable, during the night, Mary's baby was born. Mary and Joseph wrapped the baby in the swaddling bands they had brought with them. At home in Nazareth Joseph had made a cradle for the baby, but it had been too heavy to carry with them, so they put the baby, who they had called Jesus, into a manger – a wooden box in the stable that usually held hay for the animals.

King Herod was very surprised by what the wise men told him about a star and a new baby king. He was very upset. He was the king of Judea. There was no room for another one! Herod called all his advisors together and asked them, 'Where will this new king be born?' His advisors told him that the baby would be born in Bethlehem.

While all this was happening, wrote Luke, there were some shepherds nearby who were out in the fields looking after their sheep. Suddenly there was a bright light in the night sky and an angel appeared. The light shone on the shepherds and they were very frightened. The angel spoke to them. 'Don't be afraid,' said the angel. 'I'm a messenger from God. I've come to bring you good news. Today in Bethlehem a baby has been born – a baby who will be your king and your saviour. And this is what will prove it to you: if you go to Bethlehem you will find a baby wrapped in swaddling bands and lying in a manger.'

King Herod had listened carefully to what his advisors had told him. Then he had a secret meeting with the wise men from the east, and found out from them all about the star that was moving through the sky. 'Go to Bethlehem,' said Herod to the wise men. 'Go and look for this child, and when you find him, let me know, so that I may come and see him.'

The angel finished talking to the shepherds. Suddenly lots of angels from heaven appeared in the sky. The angels were singing and the shepherds could hear them. The angels sang about God's glory and God's love for the earth and all people. When the angels went back to heaven the shepherds started talking to each other about what they'd heard and seen. 'Let's go to Bethlehem,' said one of them, 'and see this baby who the angel told us about.' And they ran through the fields towards the town.

So, said Matthew, the wise men left Herod's palace and travelled towards Bethlehem. The star which had led them from the east began to move ahead of them. They were very happy.

The shepherds searched Bethlehem until they found the right stable. They saw Mary and Joseph and the baby Jesus, who had been born in the night. The baby Jesus was lying in a manger. They told Mary and Joseph what the angel had told them about the child – that he would grow up to be a king and bring people great joy.

The star led the wise men to a house where Joseph and Mary were staying. The wise men went into the house and they saw Mary and the child Jesus. They knelt down before Jesus. They knew that he would be a king. They brought out their presents and gave them to Jesus. Beautiful presents – some gold and some myrrh and some frankincense.

The shepherds told everyone they met what the angel had told them about the child Jesus. People were amazed. Mary remembered all these things and often thought deeply about them.

When the wise men left the house where Jesus was they did not return to King Herod's palace. God had warned them in a dream not to go back to King Herod so they went back to their own country by another road.

The shepherds went back to the fields outside Bethlehem to find their sheep. They sang songs to God about everything they had heard and seen. It had happened just like the angel told them.

So that's the end of Matthew's story about Jesus.

And that's the end of the story that Luke wrote down.

Sometimes when you look at pictures on Christmas cards the stories get all jumbled up.

I wonder if we can remember which story is which.

Ruth Burgess

The householder's story

Can I please make one thing clear before I really begin? I do not, never have and never will, keep an inn. Bethlehem is a one-horse town, well, maybe two or three: there's no need for a hotel, hostel or B&B. I'm a really tolerant, kindly chap, not the sort to grouse, but the end of Luke, verse seven, chapter two, should read: 'There was no room at the house.'

I'll tell you why: it was census time, all our relatives were here – just thinking about it makes me feel faint; I'm coming over all queer. Auntie Rachel says she must be careful about everything she eats – she can't touch flour or eggs or milk and is suspicious of most meats. But Cousin Dave and his wife and kids have come all the way from Rome. They'll wolf down anything if it's kosher: they're eating me out of house and home.

Brother John hates the Zealots; Uncle Dan thinks they're all right. We have to hide the kitchen knives each evening when they start to fight. I've lost count of the numbers staying – there's luggage and clothes everywhere.

Nowhere to sit, queues outside the bathroom, I'm tearing out my hair. In our bedroom there's six sleeping in the bed, seven on the floor, eight kipping down in the living room, in the kitchen four or five more. Just when I thought I couldn't take any more, along comes Cousin Joe, complete with donkey and luggage, a pregnant fiancée in tow. I could see she was in labour: she couldn't have got much fatter.

I ask you, did she want to give birth in the house, with thirty people staring at her? Children asking, 'Mummy, what is that lady doing?' At least the stable was private; it wasn't really a ruin. We threw out all the chickens, put down reasonably clean straw, the roof only leaked in three or four places, you could almost shut the door. So I think it's a bit unfair that, in every Nativity play, I'm portrayed as the nasty old villain who turned Mary and Joseph away. All right, it was dark, perhaps a bit smelly; I'll accept it wasn't much fun. But, faced with similar circumstances, what would you have done?

Brian Ford

I can talk now

It's all right
I can talk now.
For nine months I couldn't.

You've probably guessed my name.
I'm Zechariah.
You remember,
I'm a priest.
I met an angel when I was on duty in the Temple in Jerusalem
and the angel told me that my wife was going to have a baby
and I didn't believe him.

Then the angel told me that, because I didn't believe God's message,
I would be dumb until my baby was born and named,
and that's what happened.
I couldn't speak for nine months.
And when we named our baby John,
I could speak again.

Our story's strange, isn't it? –
me meeting an angel at work,
and my wife,
who's really too old to have children,
having a baby.

What do you make of what happened to us?
Can you see God at work in it?
Does it make any sense to you?

I sometimes think back to the days when Elizabeth, my wife, was pregnant.
Days of waiting,
of hoping,
days when I was really confused and afraid.
Elizabeth getting rounder and bigger,
me not speaking,
the neighbours wondering what on earth was going on,
days ... and nights ... and days.

And I remember Elizabeth's exhaustion
and our baby's birth –
it was incredible –
scary and painful and beautiful.

You know there's some quite scary bits in the Christmas stories
and I'm not just talking about King Herod.

You've probably got your tree up now
and you'll be singing carols.

If you get time
go and read our story again;
it's in Luke's Gospel
near the beginning.

I've enjoyed talking with you.
Elizabeth thinks I talk too much
but I enjoy talking.
I always have.

Thanks for listening.

Have a joyful Christmas.

Ruth Burgess, Spill the Beans

The two songs

Once upon a time you were a baby. Once upon a time everyone was a baby, even mums and dads and grannies and grandads. The baby in the Christmas story that everyone remembers is Jesus. If you look at Christmas cards there are lots of pictures of Jesus as a baby.

Look at some cards and talk about the pictures.

And there are lots of songs about the baby Jesus.

How many can you think of?

But there was another baby named in the Bible who is part of the Christmas story and not so many people remember him.

Do you remember the name of the angel who told Mary that she was going to have a baby? He was called Gabriel. And before Gabriel told Mary about baby Jesus he had been to see a man called Zechariah to tell him that his wife, who was called Elizabeth, was going to have a baby, and that their baby was going to be called John.

Before Jesus and John were born Mary went to visit Elizabeth. I wonder if they swopped stories about Gabriel – and the names that they were going to call their babies. I expect they did. I wonder what they said.

John was born before Jesus. A lot of Zechariah and Elizabeth's neighbours thought that the baby would be called Zechariah – the same name as his father. They were surprised when the baby was called John, but that was the name that the angel had told them to call him.

Mary sang a song for Jesus – a song about God's love and justice.

Zechariah sang a song too, for John – a song about God's peace and light.

In some churches people still sing these songs – Mary's song is called the Magnificat and Zechariah's song is called the Benedictus.

If you can find a quiet moment before Christmas you might like to listen to them – there's some great versions on YouTube.

Ruth Burgess, Spill the Beans

Elizabeth watches the hoopoes

They should have left long ago, but they are still here. I check every morning, though the light is weak in the courtyard, my fingers stiff and the cold latch awkward. And every morning, they are there, sitting up on the branch, their feathered crests like crowns bright in the wintering daylight. I wonder if they always stay and if I haven't noticed. Last winter, I stayed inside, barely wanting to move in case, well, just in case. I felt too old for all that growth, unready, unsteady and Zechariah was silent, so I suppose I also felt alone. The birds might have helped, had I noticed them.

My mother loved these birds, and she never would listen when my father said they were unlucky. 'King Solomon's favourites,' she'd crow. 'Confidants of the king and that shows wisdom.' But these ones in the garden can't be wise, lingering long into the winter like this. The mornings are cold now, and it takes until the afternoon for the sun to come into the courtyard.

But then, I take the boy outside to play under the tree, sitting him up on the warmed stones where we can watch the birds. They have their nest in a hole in the wall and they come and go over our heads. There are two of them, and I'm never sure which I am seeing; they are so similar. Their call makes the boy laugh. *Hoo-hoo-poe, hoo-hoo-poo.* Then their wings are a wheel of black and white, and he beams like he's seeing angels and claps his hands. He is growing so quickly now. Already pulling himself up to his feet, pushing the chair across the room. They say that boys are slow to walk, but not my boy. I shouldn't speak that aloud. It isn't fair to compare. But he is bright and we are blessed.

My thoughts are with my cousin now. She must be coming close. I wanted to be there for her, but Zechariah said it was proper to leave them be. The girl was with us long enough, he said, and there was enough talk. He doesn't understand. Yet perhaps it is all for the best. They've had to travel for this census, and, in the end, I wouldn't have been able to travel with them.

I hope she has others around her when it is her time. I had my helpers, and the midwife, too, a girl with strong arms to hold me as I quaked into that long night. She rubbed my back and helped me to sing, a low and calling melody so that he would know that the world was ready to make space for him, too. I wonder who will sing with Mary.

My mother taught me that the hoopoes are loved in Egypt, even if the priests here don't fancy them. She said they lay twelve eggs each year, small, round and blue like scraps of the sky itself, smuggled down and nurtured until the chicks can push into tender life, grow thick with feathers and fly away. I think she loved them because they are beautiful. Maybe that is enough.

Katie Munnik

Mary and Joseph

To be a good man
(Tune: 'The boar's head carol')

Chorus: Joseph learned what goodness is:
The child was God's; the care was his.

Now Joseph lived a goodly life:
a craftsman bold, who sought a wife;
and Mary long had caught his eye,
the promise made, the wedding nigh.

Chorus

But God, who chooses as he may,
stepped in and caused him great dismay:
for Mary could not hide that she
said yes to God, and pregnancy.

Chorus

Now Joseph had to face a choice:
to trust his Mary, hear her voice,
to throw her out, or else rejoice
and bear the nods, the winks, the stares.

Chorus

To foster God, our daily call:
we're called to care when neighbours fall;
when those we love are in distress,
transcend what's past to seek their best.

Chorus

May we love boldly all our days
and always walk in goodly ways.
Our thanks to Joseph and his wife –
and praise to Jesus, King of life.

Chorus

David Coleman

Advice from uncle
(Matthew 1:18,19)

Joe, Joe, don't get so stressed, boy.
I understand.
Your old Uncle Abe has been around a bit.
I can guess what happened.
A young couple in love,
a few drinks,
an evening alone together.
'Why wait till we're married?'
And the girl's in trouble.
It happens, lad, it happens.

Eh?
You're absolutely certain you're not the father?
Who is then?
Some randy squaddie from the garrison?
I didn't think she was that sort of girl.
Wouldn't say boo to a goose.
Wouldn't say no to a soldier either by the sound of it.

She's still a virgin?
A visit from an angel?
The Holy Spirit?
Oh, surely she can come up with a better story than that.

Though actually, thinking about it,
that's a very good story;
a very, very good story indeed.
Also very, very implausible.
Miracles like that don't happen round here
in Nazareth.

Brian Ford

A wee dose of reality

Immaculate conception wasn't all it's
cracked up to be.

Inside, I could hold my head up high,
knowing I had done no wrong –
but you try telling that to the old biddies
down in the market
looking for a story to gossip,
a victim to make a scandal of.

It wasn't just the dried up old widows
seething with bitterness
at their station in life,
but even the younger ones
I used to run around with.
I'd catch them, too,
blethering on the corner,
then going real quiet when I appeared –
a conversation stopper, that's me,
if ever there was one.
And who could blame them?

They saw me change from the shy bright
teenager I was, full of life,
to the sallow-skinned miserable wench,
throwing up at everyday sights and smells.
If that angel hadn't warned me,
they would have known before I did –
the signs were all there.
They'd seen them all before:
the squeamishness, the pallor.
No blooming for me;
I turned into a ghost of myself;
folk could see right through me
and they were quick to draw
their own conclusions.
They'd judged and condemned me
before I even got up to speed

and cottoned on
that what the angel said had come true:
I was pregnant.

Those serene pictures you see
of me looking calm and contented,
well – nothing could be further
from the truth!

Sure I wanted to serve God
but God had no idea what it was like
to be an unmarried pregnant teenager.
It felt like I was two different people:
a willing servant of God, on the one hand,
and a sick, scared miserable pregnant
teenager on the other.

What did God know
about pregnancy sickness,
or about stretch marks,
or about ankles that swell
and spill over your shoes,
or about developing breasts as big
and hard as watermelons?

Let's not forget the constant weariness,
and, as if all that wasn't bad enough,
there was the shunning on top.
I might be carrying God's child
but you try telling that to folk with laws
that mattered above all else,
laws that should have got me stoned.
Even the best saint would have had a job
smiling through all that,
far less a naive teenager.

Immaculate conception?
Immaculate for whom?

Liz Crumlish, Spill the Beans

Saying yes

Mary invites us to celebrate
the holy story,
to remember her song
of praise and insight,
to remember the poor lifted up,
the hungry satisfied,
the silent finding a voice.

Mary invites us to reach out,
to remember the poor of today,
the frightened, the fleeing,
the hungry and the sick,
to say 'yes' to our God,
'yes' to the travellers,
'yes' to our brothers and sisters.

Judy Dinnen

Hello, bump

Hello, bump.
No – you're not big enough to be a bump yet.
Future bump, I'm going to call you Fig.
Hello, Fig,
I know you're only tiny,
but I'm your mum.
I can't believe it.
I haven't even told anybody yet.
I don't think they'd believe me anyway.
I can't tell my mum and dad – they'll go mad!
I can't tell Joseph – he'll leave me.
I can't tell my friends –
they'll think I'm like that girl in the village:
always off with the boys, until she put on weight and wasn't seen again.
I can't tell anyone.

But I tell my angel everything.
He knows how I feel.
I know that I don't have to be afraid –
he told me not to be.
And he told me that God was pleased with me,
that God was with me.
I was frightened at first
but I wasn't frightened then.
I felt warm …
it was like a shadow came over me,
and I felt safe.
I knew God would protect me.
So any time I feel anxious I just tell my angel –
just like I'm telling you.

I'm just not sure about everyone else.
I don't know how to tell them.
Maybe I just won't say anything.
They'll find out anyway when you start to show.
They'll think it's puppy fat –
teenage hormones causing havoc with my shape.
But it's you, Fig.
It's you.

I don't know how but we'll be all right.
Even if they disown me.
Even if Joseph dumps me.
I don't need anyone else.
I've got God.
I've got my angel.
I've got you.
And I'd do anything for you, Fig.

It's funny, but when I think of you,
somehow I get what love's all about.
You aren't even born yet,
and you've already taught me love.

Louise Gough

God delivers
A dialogue between Joseph and a friend

Still not sleeping, Joseph?

Worse than that.

Worse? Nightmares?

Not exactly ... I don't know ... I had a dream.

A dream? But you don't know if it was a nightmare? Usually there's quite a difference, Joseph. Nightmares are the scary bad ones. Was it a scary bad one?

Scary, yeah, but not bad, exactly. Kind of good in a weird way, but definitely scary.

Right, what was the good bit then?

I think I've made my mind up.

Because of the good bit in an otherwise scary, weird dream?

Yep.

Right. This is making perfect sense. So what are you going to do?

I'm going to take her back. We're going to get married, just like we planned.

Brilliant, Joseph, that's fantastic. What a turnaround! You really mean it? Even after yesterday?

Don't remind me. I'll have to go back and undo that quiet word I had with the rabbi. I can't believe I did that now. I can't believe I was ready to walk out on her.

So what was the divine intervention?

I don't know if I can call it that ... it was just a crazy dream.

I seem to remember Jacob had a few of them.

I'm no patriarch.

And Joseph and Solomon and Daniel …

I'm no prophet.

Joseph, you're about to become something just as important!

What?

A dad.

Well, he'll still be half mine.

It's a boy? Brilliant! See, you always wanted a boy! Um, what do you mean 'half mine'? Is your boy going to be a prophet? Is he going to be dedicated to God like Samson and Samuel?

I … I don't know. But we've got to give him the name Jesus.

Jesus? I love it. Jesus – that means 'God delivers' – beautiful! God delivers Mary from abandonment; God delivers you from tormented indecision, and that's even before God delivers the baby to the two of you!

What have the pair of us let ourselves in for?

Oh, the gossiping will soon stop, man! Don't be afraid of that.

Don't be afraid. Don't be afraid … that was it. That was the good bit in the dream: 'Don't be afraid.'

There you go then. You're going to be a dad, and your boy's going to be something special. What's to be afraid of? God delivers! Brilliant! C'mon, let's go.

Where?

To deliver Mary from my mother's cooking. With a wee visit to the rabbi on the way …

Jo Love, Spill the Beans

My soul magnifies the Lord
(Tune: 'Wild mountain thyme')

The first three verses lend themselves to a solo female voice.

My soul magnifies the Lord
and my spirit is rejoicing,
for God is my Saviour:
He's shown favour to his servant
and holy is his name.

Chorus: He is worthy of praise.
He has shown us his mercy.
Come and worship God your Saviour,
who's shown mercy to his servant,
for holy is his name.

He has looked upon his servant,
and all will call me blessed,
for God is my Saviour:
he has done a great thing for me
and holy is his name.

Chorus

He has shown us all his power;
he will banish all injustice,
for God is our Saviour:
he will show the lowly mercy
and holy is his name.

Chorus

He has come to help his people;
he's remembered all he promised,
for God is our Saviour,
Abra'm's children's God for ever
and holy is his name.

Chorus

S Anne Lawson

'Mary – he's beautiful'

This is a story about a woman called Mary and a man called Joseph. It's also a story about two angels – angels are God's messengers – and a baby.

God sent the first angel, who was called Gabriel, to Mary with a message.

The message was that Mary was going to have a special baby.

God sent the second angel to Joseph, Mary's boyfriend, with a longer message. The message was that Mary was going to have a baby and that Joseph was to help Mary look after the baby. And … Joseph was to give the baby a special name – the baby was going to be called (can you guess?) Jesus.

Now, Mary could have said, *No – I don't want to have a baby.*

And Joseph could have said lots of No's – *no*, I won't look after Mary, and *no*, I won't help Mary look after this baby, and *no*, I won't call him Jesus – maybe I'll call him Fred!

But Mary didn't say no – she said yes.

And Joseph didn't say no – he said yes as well.

And the two angels went happily back to God; and Gabriel, who was the oldest and wisest angel, told God: 'It's good news, God – Mary and Joseph listened to your messages and they both said yes.'

So Mary and Joseph and God and the two angels all waited for the baby to arrive.

And when the baby was born, Joseph smiled and said to Mary, 'You know, Mary – he's beautiful. I'd still rather call him Fred, but I guess God knows best: we'll call him Jesus.'

Ruth Burgess, Spill the Beans

Our story

Hello, I'm Joseph. You've heard of me: I'm a carpenter; I make things out of wood and help build houses. I live in a town called Nazareth. My wife is famous, she's called Mary. She's famous because when God asked her to let him do something special, she said Yes to God. Me, I wasn't sure what I wanted to say to God ...

Listen, let me tell you our story.

Mary and I were engaged. We were in love. When we were ready we were going to get married. I was working hard to get a new house ready where we could begin our married life.

One day Mary came to me and told me that she'd had a visit from an angel. She said he was called Gabriel. He'd brought her a message from God: God had chosen her to have a baby, a special baby who would grow up to tell people about God and show them what God was like. Mary had told the angel that she wasn't married, that she wasn't ready to have a baby – maybe the angel had got her mixed up with someone else. But the angel said that his message was for a girl who'd been promised in marriage to a man called Joseph and that there was no mistake. Then the angel told Mary not to be afraid and that she would have a son and that she was to call him Jesus. Mary told me that, as the angel spoke to her, it felt like *God* was talking to her, and everything inside her wanted to say yes.

I was stunned! Amazed, frightened, full of questions, full of love and anger – all at once!

I believed Mary. Something that had made her feel good had happened to her. We loved each other: she wouldn't lie to me.

But pregnant, and it wasn't my baby, and the angel knew that we were engaged to be married ...

What was God thinking of? And why us?

When I'd calmed down I began to think about what we should do.

Maybe I should tell people that we weren't engaged any more and that we'd decided that we didn't love each other, and we weren't going to get married after all ... but that wasn't true – we loved each other lots.

Maybe I should stop seeing Mary. I could move away and start a new life somewhere else; people always need carpenters.

Maybe I should try and tell people about the messenger, the angel – but who would believe me? They'd think I was mad.

Maybe – I had lots of maybes.

And then something happened that put an end to all the maybes.

I had a visit from an angel, and this angel told me to get married to Mary because she was telling the truth. She was going to have a baby, a special baby from God, and God was asking me to help her look after him and give him his name.

The angel's visit was like a dream – but it sure woke me up!

So me and Mary had a long talk ... in fact lots of long talks. Mary had already said yes to God, and now I had said yes to God too.

We'll bring up this baby together. The angel said we are to name him Jesus. It's strange knowing already that he's going to be a boy – usually nobody gets to know if it's a boy or girl till the baby is born.

We'll look out for him, we'll make sure he's warm and fed, and we'll teach him all that we know about God, and we'll tell him and show him how much we love him. Mary's going to make him some swaddling bands and I'm going to make him a cradle.

And we're definitely going to tell him all about angels!

Why us? – we don't know – but we've made our decision: we've said yes to God – and it feels good.

Ruth Burgess, Spill the Beans

Advent thoughts from Our Lady in old age

Come, my dearest, come.
Here from before all time,
and here in time,
and gone from me,
while ever with me,
come.

Before the Father made this world –
before the Spirit's breath moved on the waters,
before light came,
you were.

Alive and active,
you the Word,
the Word God spoke,
the promise that God gave
to send and save and make us his,
or rather own that we are his.

So coming from eternity to time,
while never leaving him,
you came to me, his handmaid.

Who am I that I should mother you?

And as I waited through the months
until your birth
so now I wait for you to come again.

And as I watched you live and work beside us,
so today you live and work beside us
in the body of your church.

In my old age I wait,
as in my youth so long ago I waited.
As you came to me in time
out of eternity
so you will come and take me
to eternity from time.

Come, my dearest, come.

Anne Seymour

Shepherds and angels

Wash night
A shepherds and angels drama

Enter Shepherd 1 carrying a bucket, humming 'While shepherds watch …'. Sits down and starts washing a pair of socks in the bucket, still humming to himself.

Shepherd 2 enters calling for his lost sheep and, after noticing Shepherd 1, looks puzzled at what he's doing.

Shepherd 2: Here, sheepy sheepy! Here, sheepy sheepy! Here shee – what are you doing?

Shepherd 1: What does it look like? I'm doing the thankless task of washing the socks, and it's not easy doing it by night! I can't tell if I'm getting the grass stains out or not!

Shepherd 2: But you should be watching the flocks with the rest of us. It's not easy staying awake to keep the predators away and having people look down on you in the process. Not a lot of prospects for shepherds!

Shepherd 1: And it's more difficult for shepherds with smelly feet! Now are you just going to stand there or are you going to help?

Angel comes onto the side of the stage, at which point a bright light shines on the shepherds.

Shepherd 1: *(still washing socks and speaking to Shepherd 2)* That's the idea! Thanks for shining your light – now I can actually see what I'm doing!

Shepherd 2 is staring at the angel, open-mouthed, obviously very frightened, pointing and trying to warn Shepherd 1.

Shepherd 1: *(carries on rambling)* Well, I don't think much of this new washing powder 'Transfiguration'! It claims to get your clothes whiter than any earthly bleach could make them but it's not doing much for these socks. Do you know, they'll tell you anything these days just to get you to buy their products … What do you think? –

At this point Shepherd 1 looks up at Shepherd 2 and beyond to the angel and stops speaking out of fear.

Angel: Don't be afraid! I am an angel sent from God.

Shepherd 2: *(turns to Shepherd 1, stuttering)* Don't bbbbe affffraidddd! Don't be afraid! That's easy for him to say!

Shepherd 1: Never mind that! Look how bright his clothes are – I wonder what washing powder he uses?

Angel: When you've quite finished, I've got some news. News of great joy!

Shepherd 2: Is it this week's winning lottery numbers? … Or who's going to be the Christmas Number 1?

Angel: No!

Shepherd 1: *(excitedly)* Are they opening a 24 hour launderette in Bethlehem?

Angel: NO! This news is for the whole people. *(Angel coughs, stands up straight and then speaks as if making a formal proclamation.)* Today, in the town of David, a Saviour has been born to you: he is Christ the Lord.

Shepherd 1: Well, I don't believe it! Fancy that! A Saviour you say?

Shepherd 2: And why should we believe you? You could be one of those nutters … or someone trying to trick us so you can steal our sheep!

Shepherd 1: Or our socks!

Shepherd 2: Will you shut up about the socks!

Angel: Well, I have a sign for you: you will find a baby wrapped in swaddling clothes and lying in a manger.

Suddenly there is a chorus of voices singing Gloria (or a version played from a CD). As the music fades the angel exits.

Shepherd 1: Well, what are we meant to do now?

Shepherd 2: Let's go to Bethlehem and see this event which God has made known to us.

Shepherd 1: Well, I suppose I could leave the socks to soak for a while, but what are we going to tell the boss if we leave the sheep unattended? They might get stolen?

Shepherd 2: Let's just hope if that happens, the boss doesn't notice the villagers eating lamb chops for the next month!

Shepherds exit.

Peter Siney

Angels are special

Angels are sparkly and beautiful.

The shepherds saw angels in the sky.

Angels are special because you only see them if they want you to.

Angels sing to God.

We all have a guardian angel.

The angels sang when Jesus was born.

You have a guardian angel to protect you from people like robbers.

Mary saw an angel.

Gabriel is the chief of all angels.

When my baby is naughty the angels tell my mam.

Angels came when Jesus went up to heaven.

Angels are special.

Angels sing to God.

Primary-school children in South Shields

Come and sit

(Tune: 'Scarlet ribbons')

Come and sit upon a hillside,
see the sleeping town below.
Round the campfire, in the moonlight,
hear the tales of long ago.
How a people watched and waited,
longing for the promised King,
and the freedom and the justice
that his powerful reign would bring.

Suddenly the stars shine brighter,
music fills the cold, night air.
Shepherds fearful, awestruck, wonder;
at eternity they stare.
Heaven's riotous with rejoicing,
singing of a Saviour's birth:
seek him in a lowly manger –
God in human form on earth!

Shepherds hurry down the hillside,
led by hope, they know not where.
In an outhouse, find a baby
swaddled in his mother's care.
Prophet voices find fulfilment,
grateful shepherds glimpse God's way,
gifting to all people, all ways,
power of Love for each new day.

Avis Palmer

Angels say

Angels say – 'Don't be afraid.'
Angels mean it.
The love of God
is always stronger
than our fear.

Ruth Burgess

A shepherd's story

At first we told everyone we met,
of course we did.
It was the greatest thing that had ever happened to us.
Shepherds aren't the most respected members of society,
so to be visited by angels,
to be the first to know about the birth of a saviour –
you don't keep news like that to yourself.

Then the soldiers came.
And prudent men distanced themselves from stories about a new king.
After that everything went on as normal.
But I never forgot.
I've been on that same hillside thousands of times since,
and wondered.

Mind you, it all happened fifty years ago, at least.
Most of the blokes are dead.
There's just me and Zech left.

Then that Greek doctor turned up,
asking questions.
Seemed genuine,
gave me some ointment for my arthritis.
He'd done his homework,
talked to the mother.
So I told him everything.

Brian Ford

Something aaamazing
(For three voices)

Dress in sheepskins.

Maaa
Maaa
Baaa

My naaame is Mrs Ewe
My naaame is Granny Ewe
And I'm Mr Raaasbottom

Something haaapened to us last night
Something aaamazing
Something thaat's never haaappened before

We were up in the fields
We were up in the fields with the shepherds
And the shepherds were waaatching over us

It was a daaark night
It was a cold night
Nights are always cold and daaark in December

Maaa
Maaaa
Baaaaaa

Then something haaappened
Something aaaamazing haaaapppened
An aaaangel appeared

It was a huge aaaangel
It was a mighty aaangel
We know about aaangels. We learn about them in sheep Sunday school.

There was a light shinnning
A bright light shinnning
It was aaastounding

Our shepherds were scaared
And we were scaaared
And I was scaaared and aaafraid

And the aaangel said 'Fear not'
Yes the aaangel said 'Fear not'
And I was still scaaared and aaafraid!

And the aaangel said 'Good News'
And the aangel said 'Great joy'
And the aangel said, 'For you' … I was aaastonished

Good news for aaall sheep
Good news for rams and ewes
And even good news for the shhhhepherds

A baaaby has been born
A special baaby
Go and see the baaaby

Baaaaa
Baaaa
Maaaaaa

So we went to Bethlehem
And we found the staaable
And the shepherds caaame in with us

And we saw a donkey
And we saw some caaatle
And we found a maaanger

And there was Maaary
And there was Joseph
And there was the baaaby

A beautiful baaby
A haaapy baby
A baaaby as beautiful as a laaamb

Baaaa
Baaaa
Maaaaa

We were the first to visit Jesus
We were first to visit the baaaby
Not kings or caaamels but sheep

And we went home baaaing
And the shepherds sang God's praaaises
And we remembered the song of aaall the aaaangels

'Glory to God' they saaaid
'In the highest heaaaven' they saaaaid
'And peace on eaaarrth'

God is pleased with you
God is really pleased with you
God is walking on aaaair

Thaaaank you for listening
For listening to our story
Our story of sheep and shepherds and aaaaangels

Remember God loves alll little ones
God faaavours aaall hungry ones
God aaaamaaazingly loves aaall and every sheep

So it's goodbye from Mrs Ewe
And faaarewell from Granny Ewe
And aaadieu from Mr Raaamsbottom

Maaaa
Maaaaa
Baaaaa

Maaaa/*Maaaaa*/**Baaaaa** (together loudly)

Ruth Burgess

The story of Josh and his sheep

Before the service, hide vegetables and flowers around the building. You will need a group of cherubs who, at the appropriate place in the story, enter the building with a wheelbarrow – decorated with tinsel, an L-plate and flashing lights – and search for and collect up the vegetables and flowers.

Encourage everyone to join in Josh's rhyme (give out the words) and to count it on their fingers.

One night, one dark night, in a field near Bethlehem, there was a shepherd called Josh who was counting his sheep:

*One sheep, two sheep,
three and four,
five sheep, six sheep,
must be more,
seven sheep, eight sheep,
nine and ten,
all my sheep safe in the pen.
Phew!*

Josh often counted his sheep. They were very adventurous sheep. Only that morning one of them had wandered away from the others in search of some different food, and Josh had found her in the farmer's cabbage field! And last week, two of the sheep had got into the farmer's gardens and eaten all his flowers – they were not popular sheep.

Josh leaned back and looked at the stars, and then counted his sheep again:

*One sheep, two sheep,
three and four,
five sheep, six sheep,
must be more,
seven sheep, eight sheep,
nine and ten,
all my sheep safe in the pen.
Phew!*

It was a very peaceful winter's night. Josh liked things to be quiet. Josh was just thinking about counting his sheep again, when he heard a noise. As it grew louder he could see it was three people approaching. The three shepherds from over the hill.

'Josh, Josh,' they said, 'we're going to see a baby – you've got to come with us!'

'A baby?' said Josh, somewhat surprised.

'Yes, a baby,' said one of the other shepherds, 'the angel told us to go and see a baby.'

'An angel?!' said Josh, even more surprised.

'Yes, an angel – one that spoke – and hundreds of angels who sang,' said the other shepherd.

'Hundreds of angels?!' said Josh, more surprised than he had ever been.

'Yes, hundreds of angels – and you need to come with us to see the baby,' said the shepherd.

'I can't,' said Josh. 'I can't leave my sheep.'

'We left the dog in charge of ours,' said the other shepherd.

'But I've not got a dog,' said Josh.

They all stood still and thought a moment.

'You could ask some of the angels to look after them,' said the other shepherd. And before Josh had a chance to answer him the other shepherd shouted into the night sky: 'Angels, angels, we need your help!'

And before you could say 'Gloria', four cherubs were standing in the field by the sheep pen.

'Sorted,' said the other shepherd. 'Come on, Josh!'

But before Josh would go with them he had to count his sheep:

One sheep, two sheep,
three and four,
five sheep, six sheep,
must be more,
seven sheep, eight sheep,
nine and ten,
all my sheep safe in the pen.
Phew!

As the shepherds dragged Josh on down the hillside, the cherubs huddled up close to each other to keep warm. They'd had a long night. They'd had lots of singing rehearsals and one last flying lesson – and then they'd had to fly all the way to Bethlehem. Miles and miles and miles. The cherubs were really tired and although they wanted to help Josh they couldn't keep awake any longer, and one by one they fell asleep.

Meanwhile, inside the sheep pen, the sheep were getting restless. They'd not heard Josh's voice for a while and wondered if he'd gone away. One of the sheep put his head over the sheep-pen gate and looked around. There seemed to be some strange children fast asleep on the ground, but no sign of Josh.

The sheep were feeling adventurous: they'd not been out at night before – maybe cabbages would taste even better by starlight. One sheep lifted the latch on the sheep pen with his nose and all the sheep set off towards the farmer's cabbage field.

Hours later, as it was just beginning to get light, the cherubs began to wake up. And they soon spotted that the sheep weren't in the pen – they had disappeared! Cherubs are not supposed to panic but these cherubs did. What would they say to Josh when he came back? They'd lost his sheep!

Then one cherub had an idea. 'We could go and look for the sheep,' he said.

'And,' said another, 'if we found the sort of food they like, we could use it to get them to follow us back to the sheep pen.'

'What do sheep like to eat?' they all wondered.

'I know,' said one cherub, 'vegetables: cabbages and carrots and turnips and things.'

Shepherds and angels 249

'I've heard,' said one cherub, 'that these sheep are even fond of flowers.'

The cherubs decided they'd look for some vegetables and flowers and then come back together to see what they'd found. Off they went, in different directions. As they could fly through time and space there were lots of places they could look.

Cherubs' voices offstage:

'Where are we?'

'Which century are we in?'

'Beginning of the twenty-first, I think.'

'Wonder what sort of vegetables they grow in the twenty-first century?'

'Let's go down and look.'

'Let's try that big building – there's lights on – there must be people in there.'

Cherubs with a wheelbarrow noisily enter, searching for vegetables and flowers, which they find underneath pews, etc, with the congregation's help ... Exit cherubs with a wheelbarrow full of vegetables and flowers.

When the cherubs got back to Bethlehem they discovered that between them they'd found lots of vegetables and flowers; and one of the cherubs had spotted the sheep – they were in the cabbage field – again – and they'd nearly finished all the farmer's cabbages!

So the cherubs laid a long trail of vegetables – cabbages and carrots and parsnips and cauliflowers and even flowers – from the cabbage field back to the sheep pen, and slowly the sheep, following the long line of vegetables, came home.

'At last,' said one of the cherubs, as he shut the sheep-pen gate. 'But I'd better check that they're all here.' And he counted:

One sheep, two sheep,
three and four,
five sheep, six sheep,

must be more,
seven sheep, eight sheep,
nine and ten,
all the sheep safe in the pen.
Phew!

As the sky grew lighter, the cherubs spotted Josh coming up over the hill. As he got nearer, Josh shouted out: 'I saw the baby – he was lovely – they're going to call him Jesus. And he's a very special baby: when he grows up he's going to bring justice and hope to everyone!'

The cherubs smiled. They knew all about this baby too. They knew that the baby Jesus had been born in a stable and that God had chosen Mary and Joseph to look after him. And they knew that every Christmas night, people all over the world would meet together to hear stories about the baby Jesus and would remember how much God loved them.

Josh turned to the cherubs: 'Thank you for looking after my sheep,' he said.

'Were they any trouble?'

Now cherubs are really supposed to tell the truth, but they didn't want Josh to be worried, so one of the cherubs said: 'No trouble, Josh, they didn't move all night.'

'Ah good,' said Josh, 'they're not bad sheep really, just a bit adventurous sometimes.'

And – as the cherubs flew away into the sunlight, and the sheep dreamed of cabbages and carrots and turnips and all sorts of vegetables, and even flowers, and the baby Jesus and Mary slept safely in the stable watched over by Joseph – Josh looked over the gate of the sheep pen and smiled.

It had been a wonderful night – really special. He would be able to tell his grandchildren all about it. Who would have thought that God would have come to earth in a baby? And he had seen the baby – and the baby had smiled at him. He wanted to tell everyone how happy he was and how loved he felt. It was as if he was living in God's warm hug.

Josh yawned and stretched, and for the last time in this story he did what he was really good at ... he counted his sheep:

One sheep, two sheep,
three and four,
five sheep, six sheep,
must be more,
seven sheep, eight sheep,
nine and ten,
all my sheep safe in the pen.
Phew!

The end.

The cherubs gather up the vegetables and flowers, and stand at the church door and give them out to anyone who wants them at the end of the service.

Ruth Burgess

Glory to a child
(Tune: 'Seventeen come Sunday', Irish traditional)

I walked out on a cold midnight,
I felt the winter weather,
the sheep were huddled in the fields
to find some warmth together.
When all at once I saw a light
and I heard a great voice ringing,
singing, *Gloria*
Glory to a child
lying in a manger-o.

Here is peace, and here is life
for all the world to share in.
God pours out his love below
unbounded and unsparing.
Gifts that humble death itself
the newborn child is bringing,
singing, *Gloria*
Glory to a child
lying in a manger-o.

We went down to David's town
and found some weary strangers.
The girl was sore from giving birth,
the child was in a manger.
We sang the song the angels sang,
her face lit up like morning,
hearing, *Gloria*
Glory to a child
lying in a manger-o.

Roddy Cowie

Holy Innocents and Holy Family

Little boy in Bethlehem

Little boy in Bethlehem,
were you not just as small
and just as fragile?

Dumb bad luck
that you were born right then.

The madness of Herod
took your life
and with you, how many?
Killed
because Herod
couldn't find Jesus.

He was saved,
you were not.
Why was that?

Albert Klok

Walking to Bethlehem

Words and music by Roddy Cowie

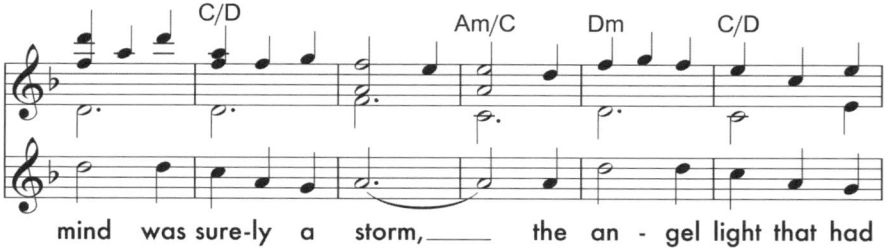

Holy Innocents and Holy Family 255

Words and music © Roddy Cowie

When Mary travelled to Bethlehem
her mind was surely a storm,
the angel light that had changed her life
and the baby about to be born at last;
and the baby about to be born.

And Joseph walking by Mary's side,
a kindly man in distress –
the place was strange, and the child not his,
but he loved her, and did what was best for them;
but he loved her, and did what was best.

When Jesus sang of a father's love,
forgiving, endlessly kind,
was Joseph walking to Bethlehem
the face that he held in his mind, and loved;
the face that he held in his mind?

Roddy Cowie

Night flight

A dialogue between two unnamed neighbours in Bethlehem

Joseph! Joseph!

What's all the yelling for at this hour of the morning?

Have you seen Joseph?

Of course I haven't. He'll still be in bed.

We've got to find him. He's got to hide the wee one.

He's got to what? Goodness, what's all that noise?

Oh no, no. They're still at it!

Who? What's going on?

Soldiers! Rampaging everywhere! They're after the children!

Nooo!

Most of us heard in time. Most of the boys are safe. Hidden. Joseph!

Oh no! Their wee Jesus! But why the children?

I don't know. Nobody knows, but they'll kill whoever they find – any of them. Joseph!

But they haven't found any of them, have they? I mean, they haven't, have they?

Yes, yes they have. Daniel and Abad, and Musa's twins, and Levi's youngest. (*Exiting*).

God help us. Nooo! Joseph!

(*Re-entering, utterly bewildered and quieter*) They're not there.

What?

They've gone. The house is empty.

Surely not.

They've taken half of what they own. In the night. They must have left in the night.

Do you think they knew? Did somebody warn them?

How could they have known? And why would they not warn the rest of us?

Where would they go?

I don't know.

Do you think they're safe?

I don't know. I hope so.

Joseph would die if any harm came to his boy. I hope he's far away and still running. I hope he never hears about Musa and Levi. I don't blame him for not stopping to think of us. If he somehow felt the danger, of course he would just pack up and run.

Maybe he left to protect us all. After all the fuss of those wealthy strangers putting the village on their map. Don't you remember how nervous Joseph got? He prayed that they wouldn't return to the palace and draw attention to a working man's house and family.

It does seem more than a coincidence – those visitors and now this. But why? Why five dear children to bury and ten grieving parents to console?

But most are safe and one has escaped.

I would have loved to see that boy grow up, you know. I can't see Joseph ever bringing him back here.

May God be with him. If he grows up to be half the man his father is, he will do well.

Jo Love, Spill the Beans

Donkey monologue

They've put me in this retirement home now. Mount Lodge, it's called. Not very original, is it? Mind you, I shouldn't complain – it's done up lovely. Beautiful stables – the decoration is impeccable. And three meals a day: carrot for breakfast, carrot for lunch and carrot for tea – not a great variety but it's always fresh, I'll give them that. And I don't mean to gossip, but some of the other donkeys in here – well, to be honest, they've seen better days. One's got a missing eye, there's a couple with water on the knee, one with a wonky ear – and another one who has got the worst case of halitosis I have ever encountered. It's enough to make you bray!

Still, all things considered, I suppose I've seen better days. My back's never been right, not since my headline-grabbing journey carrying you know who. And here at Mount Lodge I get respect for that. I'm the official top donkey, so to speak. No, when the new ones arrive it's only a matter of hours before I'm being pointed out by the others: 'Look, that one over there: that's the one that carried her all the way from Nazareth to Bethlehem.' As if I need any reminding, with a permanent curve in my spine.

Seems amazing though, that it all happened the best part of eight years ago. I'd been up for sale in this pet shop for I don't know how long. And in all that time no one had even given me a sideways glance. Then, one day, out of the blue, in comes this chap, looking a bit harassed. He comes straight up to me, gives me a quick once-over, then declares I'm perfect – exactly what he's looking for. So he pays up and off I trot, new horizons sprawling before me. Or so I thought.

When we got home, it was obvious fairly quickly we were about to take a trip. There were bags packed all over the place and no obvious spot for me to take a much-deserved rest. And just when I thought things couldn't get any worse *she* appeared: my new mistress. To describe her as 'pregnant' would be underplaying it – she looked fit to burst. And it soon became apparent that not only was I expected to carry all their worldly possessions, but her as well, bump included!

In the light of how things turned out I should be grateful for the privilege, but at the time I was seriously miffed! So would you have been. Do you know how far it is from Nazareth to Bethlehem? Well, I'll tell you – it is a flipping long way! Especially with that lot on your back.

Anyway, after travelling for goodness knows how long, we arrived in Bethlehem. The place was heaving with visitors, and of course his nibs, the Brain of Nazareth, hadn't booked us a room! I ask you! Even I know you have to advance-book accommodation, and I'm a donkey. Eventually some generous chap offers us his stable. Not particularly suitable for a pregnant woman, but for a shattered donkey it was perfect. As soon as we got in there I went to the corner and crashed out. Then I slept. And I slept like I've never slept before or since.

While I was sleeping, some amazing things apparently happened. The child was born and there were visitors from far and wide bringing greetings and gifts. But I missed it all, curled up in the corner in my coma-like sleep. Still, as my nanny always used to say, if you slept that long, you must have needed it!

When I finally awoke, I thought we might at least be spending a few days in Bethlehem, just to see some sights, but no such luck. The first thing I noticed was that all the bags were packed again, and there was even more stuff this time – what with all the baby gifts! The couple were clucking around, getting ready for the trip. I've no idea what all the rush was, but the destination, I overheard, was to be Egypt. Imagine it: Nazareth to Egypt – my poor ankles! And it was an eventful trip, full of excitement and intrigue – but I'll save that one for another day.

Ooh, look at the time! Just about ready for supper, I think. And what's on today's menu, I wonder? Looks like carrots with a garlic dip – my favourite! I tell you, there's nothing like the life of a donkey.

Jude Morton

To Egypt

We are following the path so many before us trod.
From Promised Land to Egypt …
running from danger.
Well. Not so much running as crawling.
Slow progress:
soldiers' checkpoints,
officials wanting money,
crying babies,
sobbing mothers.
Children hungry, thirsty –
but alive!
We fled Herod's men,
just in time.
Mary wept for those left behind.
I thanked God for his warning.
And so we crawled to Egypt.

Nicky Gilbert

New Year

As the old year passes
(Tune: 'Noel nouvelet')

As the old year passes
we look back, reflect:
times of joy and promise,
times we'd best forget.
God of the ages,
help us walk your way.
Help us greet your future,
seize tomorrow's day.

As the old year passes
sorrow wells within:
loved ones no more 'round us,
all that could have been.
God of compassion,
heal each ailing heart.
Guide us to your future
where new life may start.

As the old year passes
we cry for our struggling world.
Climate ever-changing,
fighting too often heard.
Jesus, you call us
to cherish all you give.
Call us to your future
where all in peace might live.

As the new year dawns now
we would give you praise.
Faithful God, come lead us
onward in new ways.
We'll love and serve you
in the faith of Christ,
in your Spirit's future:
people of new life.

David MacGregor

Got your list done?

Revelation 21:1–6a

I've been working on my list of New Year resolutions: walk more; eat more fruit and fibre, less fat; lose that 'spare tyre' around the middle (though now it is more like a complete set!). And you know what I noticed? It's the same list I had in 2015. In fact, it's the same list I had in 2005, 1995, 1985, 1975 …

It's always the same old things I am working at improving. There is no 'new' thing on my list, that activity I have never tried, that event I have never attended, that place I have never visited.

We fall into the trap of thinking God uses the same list year after year, that God will always do things the way they have always been done. Yet, the New Testament lesson we read today reminds us that God is in the business of 'newness': new heaven, new earth, new Jerusalem, new me, new you.

It shouldn't surprise us, though. Scripture makes it clear that God is always willing to risk, to dare, to think (and do) outside the box – to do something, everything new! And God wants us to be open to that new thing offered to us, to that new person who will enhance our life, to that new challenge which will make us grow, to that new opportunity we will have to serve.

So let's tear up all our old, dated lists, and be open to that one new thing (probably more, but let's start with one) that God will do for us, to us, through us.

Thom M Shuman

New year – new me

Father in heaven,
after the rush and pause of Advent,
after the whirl and joy of Christmas,
in the quiet dark tiredness of midwinter
help me to release my resolutions into your hands.
Leaning not on my own understanding,
relying not on my own strength and will,
but on your grace, your peace, your love.

Help me embrace your easy yoke
and allow myself to be re-made by you,
by the power of the Spirit,
in the likeness of your Son,
for your glory, Father God.
Amen

Evelyn Sweerts

Again we come

Another year draws to a close, Creator God.
The minutes tick away in lives lived and in hopes spoken.
How good it is to know that your words are eternal.

Another year beckons us on, God,
calls us towards it in a jumble of anticipation and fear.
How good it is to know that your presence is a reality.

Again we come, God,
to this place of sanctuary to make sense of our past and our future.
How good it is to know that your promises are everlasting.

For you have come among us as only you could,
announcing your colourful intentions
from a dull and hostile stable;
promising the world to the poor and ignorant;

asking for trouble with your talk of peace.
Inviting the world to start over.

It is our time to start over, God.
Not just with new calendars and well-intentioned resolutions.
It is time to start over with you.
The Bethlehem babe is only a week old,
yet already the bright wrappings and trappings of Christmas
have started to fade.
Angels' voices are a distant echo,
shepherds are back in their fields,
wise men have set off on new adventures
and we are relieved it's all over for another year.

Forgive our haste to leave that dirty stable
for somewhere more comfortable;
forgive our reluctance to kneel down in the dirt
and look the Christ child in the face a little longer.
Forgive our need to move on with the busyness of life
instead of lingering a while with him.
Forgive our inability to forgive ourselves
as he reaches out his arms in acceptance.

Forgive us our past, God,
renew our present
and affirm our future,
touched by your grace.

It is our time to start over, God,
and we commit ourselves to that now.
Make your home in the soiled stables of our hearts;
speak your truth in the ordinariness of our lives
and fulfil your promise in your coming among us
again and again and again
so that all may start again with you.
In Jesus' name we pray. Amen

Tina Kemp, Spill the Beans

Change me, God

Words and music by Pat Livingstone

Words and music © Pat Livingstone

New Year   269

Change me, God,
transform me …

I have written this as a flexibly scored chant. You might wish to use just No.1 as a quiet responsive chant throughout. You might wish to use one of the other versions throughout. Note: No.6 is intended as a final response.

Pat Livingstone

A liturgy of hopeful brokenness

Place pieces of pottery or sea-glass on a central table or on the floor.

Opening responses:

In hope, in love, in pieces and in peace
We come together.

In trust, in faith, in anticipation and in waiting
We stay together.

In word and silence, in naming and in knowing
We live together.

Story-weaving God, stay with us as the shadows stretch and the stars appear, as the doors close and the streets empty; amidst the wind and the waves, the stones and the sand, the calling of the geese and the lowing of the cows, come, rest with us.
Amen

Song: 'O God, you search me and you know me' (CH4 97)

Confession/Offering:

God of all that is and all that is to come, we are here to offer you our wounds of living.

**Where bodies are painful and fragile;
where remembering is heavy and haunts living;
where words and silences have hurt;
where tasks have been undone and care put aside;
where footprints have fallen heavy
and fingerprints been rough to leave marks;
where there has been breaking rather than mending;
and where, in the midst of all this,
we have denied who we are and what we can be
in your holding and birthing,
take us, cradle and hold us,
soothe and calm us
and remind us of who we are in you.**

Silence

Word

Poem/reading

Offering of ourselves:

Folk are invited to come and light a small candle from a central candle and to place it amidst the broken pieces of pottery or sea-glass.

Affirmation:

We believe in a God who cradles the soil, moulds the dust and wills flowers to resurrect amidst the paving slabs and the parched earth.

We believe in a God who lives amongst and within us and meets our brokenness in the breaking of bread, who knows the pain of living, the joy of loving and the aloneness of dying.

We believe in a God who gazes with love and compassion on all that breathes and moves, and sees starlight in our darkest and most painful places.

We affirm that we are people who live with and amidst the jagged cracks of humanity, who know the dark night of the soul, the pain of our bodies, the hurt and hope of life, and we offer all that we are and can be into the hands of the one who knows and nurtures us.

We belong to this creating, living and sustaining God. Amen

Song: 'You are the God of new beginnings', John L. Bell, from *One Is the Body*, Wild Goose Publications

Closing response/blessing:

May God bless us with new beginnings and hopeful anticipation.
May Jesus bless us with love to be a light in the darkness.
And may the Spirit bless us with the freedom to live and dream.
Amen

Fiona Barker

Bring us bright God

Bring us bright God
from yesterday
into today and tomorrow.
Cheer us with courage.
Disturb us with justice.
Safeguard us with wisdom.
Bless us with wonder.
Cherish us with love.

Ruth Burgess

God of our past

God of our past,
reconcile our brokenness.

God of our future,
renew our faith.

God of the present moment,
reach out to touch us,
and through us
the lives of all we meet
on our daily journey.

May we be made whole through
the holiness of God the Father,
the humanity of Christ the Son
and the healing power of the Holy Spirit.
Amen

Ruth Bowen

Covenant challenge

'Your will be done …
when I am disregarded,
when I lack fulfilment,
when I have nothing.'

– From the Methodist Covenant Service

If I am to say these words

I must try to trust you with a great trust.
I must try to love you with a great love.
Or else how can I say these words and mean them?

I must place my life into your hands.
I must let my heart beat in yours.
Or else how can I say these words with feeling?

I must recognise
that they are the fruit of covenant love.

Which does not make my worth dependent on myself,
what I am,
how I feel,
what others think of me,
but which makes my worth dependent on God,
who loves me for who I am,
whatever I feel like
and despite others' opinion.

And invites me to understand,
ever more deeply,
as I tentatively
offer my love and commitment.

Judith Jessop

Covenant of love
Reflections on the Methodist Covenant Service

God's never-ending love
flows on and on,
caressing with its embrace
all who let themselves
be carried along,
upheld by love.

It is not an obedient transaction.
It is not a forced commitment.
It is not a judgemental demand.

It is a willingness to be loved,
to experience the whole of life
within the love of God,

to be caught up
in passionate depths,
to learn to give
all that you are (and have)
to the One whose love
never fails.

Judith Jessop

If I had

If I had a
truck full
of faith,
I could end
all wars;

if I had a
wheelbarrow full
of faith,

I could eliminate
poverty;

if I had a
bucket brimming
with faith,
I could
build bridges
instead of walls;

if I had a
cuppa faith,
I could mend
my marriage;

but what can
I do
with this
tiny little seed
you've placed
in the palm of my
heart?

Thom M Shuman

Blessed are you

Blessed are you
now that the New Year has begun.

Blessed with the light
that overwhelms the darkness.

Blessed with the life breath of God's Spirit.

Blessed in order to bless
all those you meet on the path of your life.

Albert Klok

The 'in between' Sunday

This is the 'let down' Sunday, for the Christmas anticipation is over.

This is the 'let's take a breather' Sunday, for the New Year celebrations are still to come.

This is the 'let's give church a miss' Sunday, as we've all been so busy.

This is the 'let's look forward' Sunday, as we contemplate another year ahead.

This is the 'let's give thanks' Sunday, as we remember the past year and the fact that God has been with us all the way and will go on with us, whatever happens.

So, give thanks and sing.

Marjorie Dobson

Travelling with God
(A reflection)

Waiting for the old year to end
and the New Year to begin,
waiting to say farewell and welcome:
farewell to all that we can leave behind,
welcome to all that we travel toward.

Life in abundance is God's promise
that waits to meet us as we journey on
with a spring in our step and hope in our hearts.

Travelling with God
is never dull,
but always filled with surprises.

So we mourn not the past
nor dread the future,
but open ourselves

to the possibilities
of compassion,
of kindness,
of humility,
of gentleness,
of patience,
opening ourselves to
the possibility
of God bringing life
in all its fullness.
Hand in hand with God
we step into a brave new future.

Roddy Hamilton, Spill the Beans

God our provider
A thanksgiving on New Year's Day for 50 years of marriage

God, our provider, we give you thanks
for the many blessings of our life together
and especially on this occasion
of our golden wedding anniversary.
For fifty years of happy partnership,
we praise you for all you have given to us:
whether in good times or difficult times,
for our journeys, jobs and home life,
for the company of one another,
our common interests and diversity of viewpoints,
the doubling of joys and the halving of sorrows,
day by day, year on year, so richly blessed
by your goodness and mercy,
Light of the World, Guiding Star,
Breath of God in the eternity of love.

Terry Garley

Fresh is the morning

Fresh is the morning,
the day and the year, O God,
as we long for light
in this crossing point
between old and new,
remembered and not yet begun
story and hope.

Fresh is the morning
and our hopes with it, O God,
as we face the days,
dark now but growing ever lighter,
from solstice to summer,
frost to sunlight,
Christmas to Epiphany.

Fresh is the morning
along with our prayers, O God,
as we renew our relationship with you,
listening anew,
speaking afresh,
loving again.

Fresh is the morning.
Fresh is the year.
Fresh is the day.
Fresh is your love for us in each of them.
So be it. Amen

Roddy Hamilton, Spill the Beans

Dancing in the rain

My generation, God,
was taught that
if you couldn't afford it
you saved up until you could,
and you always put money away
for a rainy day.

It feels like the deluge
at the moment;
the world has turned around.

I would like to cling to you –
the rock that doesn't change,
but I've learnt that
everything, including you,
is always changing,
and that
taking risks
seems to be
what pilgrimage is all about.

So, God of all generations,
God of the changing years,
help me to live and love justly
and to dance in the rain.

Ruth Burgess

Epiphany

A star for our journey

(Tune: 'Away in a manger')

We come to this moment, we have travelled so far,
like long ago wise men who were led by a star.
The roads we have taken are the days of the year,
and some have been joyous and some full of fear.

We come to this moment, we come as we are,
with all that has happened we bear the year's scar.
But here there is welcome, no more need we roam:
in the birth of the Christ child our hearts have come home.

This moment's eternal, it's endlessly new,
God's presence amongst us is endlessly true.
How awesome the silence in which can be heard
the hope and the peace of the incarnate Word.

This moment's to treasure, it's wonder, it's praise!
Enthralled by such gifting, we can only gaze.
How small is this life-light, how bright and how clear,
a star for our journey as year succeeds year.

Avis Palmer

Star of wonder

I wonder …

as she cleaned up
the barn,
packing for the trip
to God-only-knows-where
was Mary muttering
under her breath,

'Men!
they couldn't have
brought diapers,
or given us
a crib?'

As he pulled
and begged the donkey
to stand still while
the bags were loaded on,
did Joseph think,
'Wise?
They couldn't figure out
I could have used
a new power drill,
or at least some
of that Persian hardwood
that is rarely in the store?'

When we reach out
to gift those in need,
are we wise enough
to provide what
they really need,
a job,
childcare,
a clinic,
a friend?

I wonder …

Thom M Shuman

We all have gifts

Joe sits on the pavement playing his flute, cap in front of him, his dog Barney lying beside him, snoring gently in time to the music.

Everyone has gifts, Joe says to himself, remembering his Sunday-school days

But I have nothing to offer to anyone: I am homeless, live in a hostel, have no job, and own nothing except the flute my music teacher gave me years ago – and of course Barney.

A lady passes by and drops a few coins into his cap, 'What lovely music you are playing!' she says.

At the end of the afternoon he packs up his stuff, and with Barney sets off to the hostel. As they make their way it starts to pour with rain. He passes an elderly lady wearing no coat, getting very wet; he takes off his jacket, puts it around her shoulders, and continues on his way.

Everyone has gifts.

Katherine Rennie

Mary remembers the visitors

So many curious eyes eager to see this child.
Burly-bearded shepherds looming in that small space
awestruck as they stare at my baby.
Large, rough, calloused hands take him
and cradle him with amazing gentleness.
Slow smiles give way to joy as the angel's words are repeated,
dreamy faraway looks as they recall celestial songs.
Then they depart bubbling with a joy that they long to share.
And later there is the rustle of silk and a whiff of incense
as tall regal men kneel before my child
and solemnly present gifts fit for a king.
The star has brought them to journey's end
and yet really their journey is only just beginning.

Elizabeth Clark

Epiphany 285

We use our gifts for God

Words and music by Ruth Bamforth

Words and music © Ruth Bamforth

We use our gifts for God.
We use our gifts for God.
When things go right, when things go wrong,
we use our gifts for God.

Ruth Bamforth

Other verses: 'We keep our faith in God.' 'We put our trust in God.'

We are

This script needs a minimum of five speakers, but would be better with a few more so that you have multiple voices for the Magi and Advisors.

Magi:	We are the astrologers. We watch the stars in the heavens. One star has got us excited. We have followed it for a long time.
Herod:	I am King Herod. I am strong and powerful. I live in a palace in Jerusalem. No one messes with me.
Advisors:	We are the king's advisors. We study books about God and history. King Herod frightens us. We tell him what he wants to hear.
Mary:	I am Mary. I am staying in Bethlehem. I have a baby called Jesus.
Star:	I am a star.
Magi:	We are the astrologers. We have arrived in Jerusalem. We have been to the palace and have spoken with the king.
Herod:	I am King Herod. I have heard about a baby. An important baby. No one is going to be important around here but me.
Advisors:	We are the advisors. We told Herod what we have read in our books: that a baby, born in Bethlehem, will grow up to be a king.
Mary:	I am Mary.

	I am looking after Jesus. He is smiling this morning.
Star:	I am a twinkling star.
Magi:	We are the astrologers. We are going to Bethlehem. Herod has told us the child will be there.
Herod:	I am King Herod. I have sent the astrologers to Bethlehem and told them to come back to me and tell me where this child is!
Magi:	We are the astrologers. We have found the child. We have given him some presents. Do you know what they were? *(optional space for participation)*
Mary:	I am Mary. We have had some visitors. They brought Jesus some strange presents.
Star:	I am a beautiful twinkling star.
Herod:	I am King Herod. I am waiting for the astrologers to return to my palace and tell me where the child is.
Magi:	We are the astrologers. We are not going back to King Herod. He is the stuff of nightmares. We are going home another way.
Mary:	I am Mary. I am still looking after Jesus.
Star:	And I am still a beautiful twinkling star.

Ruth Burgess, Spill the Beans

Wise

When the star arose
there was much excitement among the gazers
about what it might mean
and how to explain its appearance.
They wanted it named, and claimed.

But our hearts were beating faster
because to us it was captivatingly,
beautifully
more
than could be pinned down by definitions
(as if words could tame it!).
What was (visible, predictable, definable, comprehensible)
served only to make us aware of
something else
that was not.
We travelled, we followed, we enquired,
we found the baby.
Our journey took us home; the star faded.
Reports made, case closed.

But our hearts would never again beat without that rush of
hope-life-fear-joy
that we knew
when we first saw that star,
which redefined with one glimmer of light our life's meaning.

What captivated us then has continued to elude our rational comprehension
but its wordless and indefinable call
is, still, an insatiable yearning
to seek beyond what can be found,
to gaze through what can be seen,
to ask more than can be answered,
and to worship.
And so we live
for what was embodied there that day.

Anna Bosatta

A bright light is shining
(Tune: 'Brightest and best')

On the horizon a bright light is shining,
calling on magi to travel afar,
leaving behind all the known and familiar,
risking their future to follow a star.

Harsh is the way, very long is the journey,
crossing the borders of custom and doubt;
seeking a new prince, not found in a palace,
what has this pilgrimage been all about?

Led to the stable, they're filled with elation:
God is revealed in a small baby's face.
Humbled, they're kneeling in silent devotion,
sensing within an outpouring of grace.

Gold is presented and laid on the stone floor,
costly and precious, a gift for a King;
ruling his people with love and compassion;
freedom and justice, Christ's Kingdom will bring.

Incense, so rare, is placed gently beside him,
fragments of fragrance, a gift for a priest;
lifting the prayers and the hopes of his people,
valuing those who are poorest and least.

Myrrh is the last of the wealth to be offered,
oil for embalming, a gift for his death;
sold and denied, he will know crucifixion;
love will be shown 'til his very last breath.

Magi head homewards with no star to follow,
finding new meaning, it's hard to depart.
Christ is for seekers, he still journeys with them.
Christ is for all who have given their heart.

Avis Palmer

Strangers at the door bringing gifts
(A prayer for refugees and asylum seekers)

Do we hear the knocking at the door?
Do we open the door?

Are we afraid?
Or are we ashamed the house is a mess?

Do we welcome in the stranger?
Do we recognise the gifts they bring?
Do we trust their story?
Do we accept the gifts they have brought from afar?
Do we allow them to change us?
Do we realise that only by opening the door
will we recognise the true Christ,
the God who is hidden in smallness,
who arrives in unexpected places, at unexpected times?

Do we hear the knocking at the door?
Who will open the door?
Who will open the door?

Fiona van Wissen

The wise of old

The wise of old had their epiphany;
a star shone in the heavens.
They searched
and found their fulfilment.

The foolish of today
look for a star in human guise;
they search
and seldom find what they seek.

We need to become wise again.
The wise still seek Him.
They seek Him,
not any lesser star
but the One who rules over the stars in the heavens.

Pam Hathorn

Those first visitors

When those first visitors came to you, Lord,
they brought gifts to lay at your feet.
But it was they who left the richer for having seen you.

Our gifts are not those of kings
but we offer them now
with that same awe and expectation
believing they, as we, may be worthy
to be used for your work in the world.

We are not as wise as we would like to be,
yet we offer you ourselves,
all that has gone before and all that lies ahead,
in your service.

As we lay what we have
and what we are before you,
may our eyes look heavenward,
may our hearts rise in expectation
and may we, together,
be instruments of change and bringers of light
in places of need.
In Jesus' name we pray.
Amen

Tina Kemp, Spill the Beans

WOW!

Long, long ago in a land far away, three men were watching the stars. Every night they looked up into the sky and the stars changed. Sometimes the stars seemed to make patterns and the men gave them names. Sometimes one star twinkled more brightly than another.

One night, a new star appeared in the sky. It was bright and it seemed to be moving. The men were excited. They wondered if the star was trying to tell them something.

The next night the star was there again, very bright, and it had moved a bit more across the sky.

'It's calling us,' said one of the men, whose name was Melchior.

'Maybe it wants us to follow it,' said another man, who was called Caspar.

The third man, who was the youngest and had the longest name, Balthazar, just said, 'WOW!'

The men talked to each other all night. They looked at their books to see if they could find out anything about the new star. And one of their books told them that a new star would appear in the sky when a new king would be born.

'Shall we follow the star and see where it leads us?' said Melchior.

'Sounds a good idea to me,' said Caspar.

Balthazar rubbed his hands together, and just said, 'WOW!'

'If it is a new king we'll need to take him presents,' said Melchior.

'And we'll need lots of food for the journey,' said Caspar.

Balthazar rubbed his tummy, and just said, 'WOW!'

It took them a few days to get everything ready, but the star kept shining in the sky, almost as if it was waiting for them.

At last they were ready to go, and they set off, at night, with the star leading the way.

They went across deserts.

They went through towns.

They crossed streams and rivers.

And the star kept moving in the sky.

One night they got the map out.

'It looks like we're here, by this village,' said Melchior, pointing.

'It looks like we're moving towards Jerusalem,' said Caspar.

Balthazar stood up and turned round in a circle, and just said, 'WOW!'

A few nights later, they found themselves in Jerusalem, which was a huge city, and the star stopped moving.

'Now what do we do?' said Caspar.

'If we're looking for a king, we'd better try the palace,' said Melchior.

Balthazar opened his eyes wide and looked all around him, and just said, 'WOW!'

They had to ask the way to the palace, and people told them that a king called Herod lived there, and he was not a very nice king, in fact he was really nasty.

'We'd better be careful what we say,' said Caspar.

'And we'd better say it nicely,' said Melchior.

Balthazar hid his face behind his fingers, and whispered, 'WOW!'

They went into the palace and they talked to King Herod and told him all about the star and their journey. Herod seemed interested, but when they told him that they thought that the star might be leading them to a new baby king, Herod looked very cross. Herod talked to people in his palace, and they agreed that the star might be pointing to a new baby king, and their books said that the baby might be born in Bethlehem, a village about five miles away.

Herod went back to Caspar, Melchior and Balthazar and told them to keep following the star, and if it led them to a baby, they were to come back to his palace and tell him all about it.

As they went down the palace steps Caspar said, 'He was a bit scary.'

And Melchior said, 'Very scary.'

And Balthazar nodded, and very quietly he just said, 'WOW!'

The men looked up into the sky and the star was moving again and they followed it and found themselves on the outskirts of the village of Bethlehem.

'Seems a strange place for a king to be born,' said Caspar.

'I don't think there are any palaces here,' said Melchior.

Good job, thought Balthazar, who was stamping his feet to get warm.

There were no palaces in Bethlehem, just houses and shops, an inn, some stables. The star moved across the village and stopped and it seemed to be shining on one building.

'This must be it,' said Caspar.

'Let's go and look,' said Melchior.

And Balthazar smiled and changed his word, and this time he shouted, 'NOW!'

The star was shining over a small house.

They knocked on the door and a young woman opened it and invited them in.

And there, in a basket, was a baby, a baby who was wide awake and looking at them and waving his little arms in the air.

'He's beautiful,' said Caspar.

'We've got presents,' said Melchior.

And Balthazar clapped his hands and the baby laughed, and Balthazar smiled and smiled.

They stayed a long time, talking to the lady, and smiling at the baby, and all too quickly it was time to go.

They stood outside the house, and it seemed as if someone was whispering to them – *'Don't go back and tell Herod about this baby'* – so they didn't.

'We've had a great adventure,' said Caspar.

'We'll go back another way,' said Melchior.

Balthazar stretched and yawned; he was really tired. There was only one word left for him to say to finish this story, and Balthazar just said, 'WOW!'

Ruth Burgess, Spill the Beans

New roads

When the star had stopped
and they had seen the baby
they took a new road.

When the decorations come down
and we have heard the story
we can take a new road.

New roads can be scary.
New roads are exciting.
New roads are risky.
It is time to go.

Star-maker,
Light-bringer,
Holy Spirit of adventure,
come with us this *morning/evening* on our road. Amen

Ruth Burgess

Homelessness Sunday

We belong to God

Generous God, we thank you for places to call home,
and for journeys that carry us to special places and special people.

We pray for those who have no choice
but to gather the scattered pieces of their lives and their families
and carry their story into a new place.

We pray for those for whom home is no longer a safe place,
for those who look for sanctuary and safety
on the streets and across borders.

In safety or in danger,
we belong to God.

Wealthy or poor,
we belong to God.

Human, deeply human,
we belong to God.

Fiona Barker

Walking by the homeless

As we bundle on layer upon layer of warm clothing,
may we not become so cocooned as to
turn blind eyes and ears to those in need.

As we prepare for winter feasts,
may we share with those who are hungry.

As we turn up the heating in our homes,
may we remember those without shelter,
and not just remember,
but open wide the doors of welcome.

Fiona van Wissen

May our hearts and minds be open

Opening responses:

God, source of life and abundant love,
We gather to praise and worship you.

God, wellspring of goodness and amazing grace,
We gather to praise and worship you.

God, essence of justice and eternal joy,
May our hearts and minds be open to your healing touch.

God, heartbeat of hospitality and never-failing hope,
May our hearts and minds be open to your healing touch.

Prayer:

Living God, within whose loving purpose each and every one of us has a valued place – is welcomed, the very hairs of our heads numbered – we confess that too often, when things are going well, we take our good fortune for granted, and we are blind to the needs of others. And so we pray that we may be content with enough and may be generous towards those who lack money, food or shelter.

Jesus Christ, in whose way we seek to follow, who had a special concern for people on the margins, we confess that too often we have passed by the beggar in the street, the *Big Issue* seller, the person who needed our compassion. And so we pray for victims of poverty, people who are homeless, those who are struggling to cope, and all who seek to help and support them.

Holy Spirit, permeating life, guiding us, comforting us, challenging us, we confess to our share and complicity in the failings of a society where the gap between rich and poor is still so wide and there is a desperate need for more affordable housing. And so we pray that leaders within national and local government may develop creative and compassionate policies and that all organisations and people who strive for housing and economic justice may be faithful to their task.

Norman Shanks

Winter

Dilemmas

Words and music by Ruth Bamforth

1. Choi - ces are hard to make. Deci - sions are hard to take. Where there's cheat-ing, ly-ing, bul-ly-ing, what do you do?
2. Choo - sing what's wrong or right, decid - ing which cause to fight, for the hun-gry, home-less, des - ti - tute, what do you do?

Words and music © Ruth Bamforth

Homelessness Sunday

302 Winter

Homelessness Sunday 303

Choices are hard to make.
Decisions are hard to take.
Where there's cheating, lying, bullying, what do you do?

When to speak out, and when to be silent?
When to stand up for what you believe?
Have you the courage of your convictions ...
to follow His lead?

Choosing what's wrong or right,
deciding which cause to fight,
for the hungry, homeless, destitute, what do you do?

When to speak out, and when to be silent?
When to stand up for what you believe?
Have you the courage of your convictions ...
to follow His lead?

Jesus knew when to speak;
He championed the poor and weak,
wanting fairness, justice, equality – we want them too!

So show me:
when to speak out, and when to be silent,
when to stand up for what I believe;
give me the courage of my convictions ...
to follow Your lead,
to follow Your lead.

Ruth Bamforth

Winter in January

As the sun revives

God of all seasons,
in the dreich, wet, cold and windy days of winter
our spirits long for the warmth and comfort of spring.

As the sun revives
and brings life to the whole of creation
so we long to be part of that renewal and rebirth.

Hear our prayer for the reawakening of hope and love and peace
in ourselves and in the world.

And hear our songs of gratitude and praise
as we join together with one voice
in the universal song of love.

Katy Owen

God of ever-new beginnings

God of ever-new beginnings,
God in whom past, present and future perpetually coalesce,
as a new year unfolds before us,
through the dark days of January,
through the vagaries of the weather,

though storm, flood, ice or snow may unsettle us,
though personal difficulties may beset us,

help us always to remember
that your light shines through the deepest darkness,
that your love surrounds and summons us,
that your life is stronger than death itself,

and that your grace sustains us
and is sufficient for all our needs.

Norman Shanks

A litany of hope

As long as the earth endures, seedtime and harvest, cold and heat, summer and winter, day and night, shall not cease. Genesis 8:22

The trees of the wood await spring's re-clothing;
the branches will be green again:
This we affirm: God is faithful and true.

The sun will rise higher in our skies;
its light will be warm upon our faces once more.
This we affirm: God is faithful and true.

The days will grow longer;
light will push back the darkness.
This we affirm: God is faithful and true.

Seeds will germinate and grow;
the flowers will bud and bloom.
This we affirm: God is faithful and true.

The ears of the wheat will form and ripen;
the grass will grow to feed the cattle.
This we affirm: God is faithful and true.

Swallows will return and fill the skies;
birds will fill the land with song.
This we affirm: God is faithful and true.

Simon Taylor

Angel in the dump

Any home gardener knows that an unseasonable warm snap in January will wreak havoc on perennials and spring bulbs. So, I put 'Mulch the beds' on my To Do list and drove to the dump, the best source of fresh mulch in our area. It's also, in mid-January, a green-and-brown monument to the Christmas just past.

I am not Catholic, nor was my grandmother, although she always insisted that she once saw the Virgin Mary appear at the foot of her bed. So, I must have a special spiritual eye for glimpses of ...

Well, here is a poem I wrote when I returned home after a remarkable, grace-filled moment in that vast dump site.

Like children,
snowdrops, daffodils and crocuses
need protection from
January warmth that betrays
a bitter cold to come.
Day after warm day, the sun seduces their
green tendrils to grow taller.

A trip to the dump for mulch to blanket
these naive thrivers reaps a surprise.
Christmas trees that recently displayed the
joyous lights celebrating the Nativity
now are piled like matchsticks awaiting the grinder.
They have no memory of the joy they pretended
nor the innocence they invoked.

A bright colour embedded in crushed branches lured me to one tree.
Tucked amidst still-fragrant boughs –
green paper-cone Scotch-taped for body,
red rough-cut wings,
white circle for a face –
a handcrafted angel.

And deeper I peered, the crayon words:
'Angle Mary protekt us from guns.'

A child's prayer discarded with this tree.
Maybe by mistake?
Snagged in the branches as they went.
Now, an Angel in the Dump,
a plea for all the innocents
whom we discard from our memories,
from our prayers.
So quickly.
I replaced the boughs around her.
Tucked her in. Echoed the prayer:
Protekt us all from guns.

Benjamin Pratt

That name
Exodus 3:14

Snowflakes multiply
white upon white
into winter's brighter shadow.
It's Monday, and the day
grows old with coffee
and numbers,
and the stale words
with which I limp home.

Later, on the stoop, as I stroked the dog, a hush
descended and a spreading purple stain
began swallowing the sunset.
The quiet now begun, deepened, and soon, hitched
to every flake, one by one, thousands upon thousands
grew an assemblage of silence greater than anything I knew,
deeper than thought, than snow, as deep as God.

And so I felt free at last to use that name, somehow guessing
there was in the accumulation of these fragile, icy stars
all the warmth I'd ever need.

Marc Harshman

Winter in January

312 Winter

Lord, we give thanks for cre-a-tion.

Lord of the winter, enfolded in night,
darkness wrapped round the brief hours of grey light,
waves rush the shore and break icy and white,
the moorlands are dark desolation;
stripped of their softening colours we see
starkness and strength in the limbs of the trees,
storm clouds throw back what they swept from the sea:
O Lord, we give thanks for creation.

Lord of the springtime and green-tinted trees,
blue and grey sky and a sharp-fingered breeze,
young lovers happy to chatter and tease
and birds going wild with elation;
wildflowers nodding on plots of bare ground,
evenings when children can shout and run round,
rain on the river's great rustling sound:
O Lord, we give thanks for creation.

Lord of the summer, the sun in its pride,
cool shadowed places to rest and to hide,
small flies and beetles that scuttle and fly
and liven the air with vibration;
meadows with blossoms red, purple and gold,
rocks bask in dreams half a billion years old,
round them the sea pushes, restless and cold:
O Lord, we give thanks for creation.

Lord of the autumn, the rowan shines red,
fat brambles gleam round an old broken shed,
young swans still brown arch their elegant heads
and swim in their stately formation;
out in the fields there is barley and wheat,
one day you relish it, nutty and sweet,
next day, sharp stubble spikes under your feet:
O Lord, we give thanks for creation.

Lord, you lay on us the duty of care:
we point this place towards life or despair;
help us to carry the burden we bear
and not to become its destruction;
one sphere of life in the vastness of space
balanced and fragile, alight with your grace:
Lord, let us serve you by serving this place
and truly give thanks for creation.

Roddy Cowie

At the pantomime

Mid-January, Saturday afternoon.
The village hall is packed with children
for the pantomime matinee.
It's *Beauty and the Beast* this year.
The Dame is in a haunted house
(if you are asking how or why
then you don't understand pantomime).
She doesn't know where the ghost is
and repeatedly asks the children to tell her.
'It's behind you!' they bawl.
But every time she turns round it ducks
and (somehow) she doesn't see it.
Four score children are on their feet shrieking
and screaming in delighted frustration.
(Some have to rush out to the toilet to avoid wetting themselves.)
How can an adult be *soooo* stupid?
The scriptwriter has slipped into the hall
and sits quietly at the back with the sound and lighting crew,
still amazed that his words –
dead, black marks on flat white paper –
have sprung into life
and made such a world of innocent happiness,
of excitement and thrills,
where the righteous,
despite lapses into total stupidity,
will win in the end.
He has tasted the addictive joy of creating.
Would it, he wonders, be blasphemous to say,
'Behold it was very good'?

Brian Ford

January dawn

Dawn, sunrise,
a mystical, magical moment
that holds
a new day
in its grasp.

Sunrise in January
is special,
earlier each morning,
scattering darkness
in the gloomy days of winter,
promising light,
warmth
for this day.

The light spreads,
creating patterns
of clouds,
changing, whirling
into new shapes.

But we don't know
what any day will offer,
how any day will develop.
For some of us
this will be an adventure.

For some of us, radical trust.

Jean Hudson

Winter walk on Hod Hill

My boots crunch
as over the earth's crusty frost
I conquer the hilltop path.

A man approaches with a dog.
We nod polite recognition.
A thousand cawing crows
rise from skeleton trees.

The sun slips down the sky.

I descend through the twilight.

Distant ducks are shuffling to bed,
an impatient owl is hooting –
my heart sings.

I look forward to
a roaring log fire,
a pot of hot tea
and a large slice of homemade cake.

Tricia Creamer

The first time

The first time
I went to Camas*
was in January.

I'd only lived on Iona
a month,
and had struggled
with the 5:30am ferry.
That was madness.
This was beyond words …

Torch-lit
in mid-afternoon
we staggered down the track
with our bags packed
ready to travel
the next morning
to the staff reunion
in Edinburgh,
or was it Glasgow?
Safe indoors
we moved as close as possible
to the fire.

Later someone suggested bed
'It'll be a long day tomorrow'
and attempted to show me
to a shed!
I stayed by the shrivelling flames
wrapped in my sleeping bag.

I was woken early,
cold piercing my bones,
and was given the job
of escorting a goat
(who sensibly didn't
want to leave its stable)
up the track
in the dark
to a waiting minibus.

I can't remember
how many goats
we were taking with us.
I think it was two.
It felt like a herd.

Into the minibus climbed
six adults,
could have been more,

two children
plus two goats.

(Rustle a crisp packet
any flavour
and goats will follow you anywhere.)

What can I say of the journey?
It was long.
Goats are not minibus-trained.
Goats do not wear nappies.
Goats urinating in a warm, enclosed, moving space,
make adults and children
feel
and be
sick.
And goats will chew anything,
especially anything that might,
to a goat's mind,
contain crisps.

As we began to enter
the city
we were spotted by
adults
children
car drivers
taxi drivers
bikers
passengers
bus drivers
and an assortment of dogs.

The goats seemed to enjoy this.

And I may be wrong
but I recall that
every traffic light we drew up to
was on red.

Hours –
or was it days? –
later,
I reached my destination
and escaped.
The goats travelled on
to some haven of
crisp production in the sun.

Having heard my story
you will understand my mixture of memories
when I am asked
if I have ever been to Camas.

Happily I have been back since
in summer,
under blue skies
with the midges biting …

But it is
the memory
of that first freezing January night
and ensuing day,
and the smell of
warm
urine-soaked
hay bales
that pungently
remains.

Crisp anyone?

Ruth Burgess

* Camas is the Iona Community's Adventure Centre on the Isle of Mull.

A communion liturgy

In the beginning, Breath poured forth
and goodness was born,
bringing Light from darkness,
life from chaos,
birth from the Womb of Creation.

Circling round the fire,
from the beginning of humanity,
people gathered to tell their story and to give thanks
for the gifts of the Creator:
promise of seed,
hope of new life,
wholeness of heart,
sacredness of all that lives and breathes.
And the creatures, in their own language, spoke their gratitude:

The world is full of your goodness and mercy.
We give thanks today, tomorrow and always.

In the fullness of time
goodness was once again born,
and the world came to know our brother Jesus,
born of woman, whole in heart and Spirit,
dedicated to the Way of God,
who invited all to the table of grace and continues to invite us now
to this circle of healing and hope.

As he gathered his disciples in his time,
we come now to remember and seek to become
the Body of Christ in our own time.

This bread, gift of earth, promise of seed, is prepared for all to share.
Eat with thankful hearts and hope of life renewed.

This wine, gift of the Vine that connects us all,
is offered with joy and celebration.
Seed and fruit given to feed our hunger and quench our thirst.

These offerings bind us together in this eternal life-giving act.

Creator, Christ, Sacred Spirit,
fill this meal and this circle with the gifts of life
so we may be seed and fruit for one another and all creation,
for the nourishment of all.

With all of creation we continue to say:

The world is full of your goodness and mercy.
We give thanks today, tomorrow and always.

As Jesus remained true to the goodness and mercy planted within him,
even till death,
may we live lives that help to feed the hunger
and quench the thirst of the world.

May we also offer ourselves, as Jesus did,
as gifts of healing through our words of love and our acts of justice.

O God, may we continue to welcome to the circle all who are in need
and share in our awe and thanksgiving saying:

The world is full of your goodness and mercy.
We give thanks today, tomorrow and always.

Let us pray together:

Our Creator,
who dwells in heaven and earth,
sacred are all your names.

May your circle of mercy and care be present this day and
your will for all creation bring us into your light,
even as we are held by your great love throughout time.

Feed us today with the gifts of your goodness
and bathe us in your mercy,
as we offer acts of justice and love to all we meet.

Help us to turn from all that leads us from your way
and save us from all that destroys life.

For this creation is yours,
full of awe and beauty and mystery,
today, tomorrow and always,
may it be so, Amen

Sally Howell Johnson

January 28th

Accommodating
this unaccustomed,
killing cold
has been like living
in a Russian novel.

Hoarfrost on windows
distorts light reflected
from un-melting snow.

The air glitters
with tiny bits of ice,
minute shards of glass
that cut when breathed.

Quivering tufts of fluff,
small birds shelter
in the wood pile.

God knows what
becomes of our homeless.

On Holy Name Day
I planted a gift
of paper-whites,
six bulbs in two deep pots.

Today four swelling buds,
eight elegant blossoms

grace the chill drafts
of this hermitage
with fragrance finer
than any tsarina's
precious French perfume.

Bonnie Thurston

Winter hope

Giver of life and strength and hope,
when the winds rage and the rain pours,
damaging this world with persistent force;

when land moves and rivers rise
to destroy homes, roads, livelihoods or lives;

when darkness above covers the skies
and nature goes beyond our bounds;

lead us to calm our ways and heal our wounds;
renew our will to protect and restore the earth
from the degradation of over-exploitation
to feed our desires.

Guide us into wisdom,
restraint and care for this planet, our home,
that we may use it gently to supply our need,
free from the extravagance of pursuing greed.

Terry Garley

Turning the sod

Sharp plough glinting in the sun
turning dull bare earth
preparation for a new start
a nourishing seedbed
new beginnings
new life
new growth

Holy Spirit, sharp ploughshare for our hearts
turn the dull bare earth of our lives
preparation for new starts
nourish us with your word
prepare us for
new beginnings
new life
new growth

S Anne Lawson

The baptism of Jesus

He scared me

He scared me.
He did.
With his words,
with his stories.
John they called him.
He scared me
and yet he held me.
I wanted to hear what he had to say.

He said he was not the one the old stories talked about.
He was not the Messiah.
He was a messenger
to tell us that the Messiah was coming soon.

He talked about fire
and he talked about judgement.
He baptised people in the river,
and told them to change their ways.

I listened to him from a distance.
I was not going to go any nearer.
He scared me
and yet he held me.
I still wanted to hear what he had to say.

And then I saw a man wade into the water,
and before John ducked him under
they stood and talked to each other.
I couldn't hear what they said.

When John baptised him
something happened –
there was a bird and a voice from nowhere,
a voice we all heard.

Well done, Jesus.
You are my son.
I love you.
*With you I am well-pleased.**

It was weird
but really powerful.
Nobody who saw and heard it
would ever forget that day.

He scared me, did John,
with his stories of fire and judgement.
He scared me
and yet he held me
and I wanted to hear
what he had to say.

*This could be read by a different voice.

Ruth Burgess

Am I ready?

Am I ready, Father?
Ready to face the world:
to start a new career
of shaping people's lives
as I shaped the wood
in the workshop.

Am I ready, Father?
Ready to face the factions
clamouring for a deliverer,
a healer, a miracle worker,
a fixer of all their problems.

Am I ready, Father?
Ready to confront the sickness and evil,
the arrogance of the professional
peddlers of religion,
the obtuseness of friends and family.

Am I ready, Father?

The dove of peace descends
and I rise from the waters,
cleansed, cooled and calmed.

I'm ready, Father.
Ready as I'll ever be.

Carol Dixon

What did it for me

A: It was the locusts.

B: It was the water.

C: It was the repentance.

A: He came out from the desert.

> He just came walking out of that wilderness, with roasted locusts in his hand, sticky with honey, and he wrapped himself in camelhair skins. That's what did it for me, that set him apart.

B: He stood there in the water of the Jordan inviting us all in.

> Anyone and everyone, no fear of the authorities standing there with smirks upon their faces trying to make him look a fool. That's what did it for me.

C: He shouted at everyone: 'Repent!' Really shouted.

> It wasn't some polite invitation but an urgent call that was meant to frighten us as well as invite us.

> It was his shouting that did it for me.

A: He looked like a madman and sounded like a prophet. I'm not sure there is much difference between the two. But everything about him, his wild honey and locust diet, his clothing, his mad eyes, all spoke about someone who wasn't going to toe the line with Israel's religious authorities, all properly dressed in their finery. He spoke with authority, more than the rest. But it wasn't about him. He spoke of someone greater than him coming after him.

B: The water seemed so inviting. He made it inviting, to be washed clean, but not from the dirt of the desert but from the dirt of my past. Baptised. Yet he spoke, and he warned us that while it was water for the moment, the one coming after him would baptise with fire and the Holy Spirit instead. And I couldn't help myself but trust him, and I went into the water and was washed by him: the past fell away and I was clean again to live life anew.

C: His words were urgent. 'Repent!' he said, and I did. Oh yes, I repented of everything. Once I started talking I didn't stop. I was taken along by the whole thing, and I confessed everything I could remember. 'Repent!' he said like it was the most important thing I could ever have done. There was no other place in my faith to do this. No cleansing greater than this. But this wasn't about him. I was ready now for the next one coming after him. I was prepared to listen anew.

A: It was the silence.

B: It was the water.

C: It was the voice.

A: He came out from the crowd and stood in the water facing John.

B: He came out of the water and stood facing heaven.

C: He came out of himself and smiled as if he heard a voice.

A: You are my son.

B: The beloved.

C: With you I am well-pleased.

A: It was the moment.

B: It was the time.

C: He was the One.

Spill the Beans

To live out our baptism promise

God, so often in baptism
we celebrate the gift of new life:
life that is conceived in love
and received with joy.

Our children are, on the whole,
nurtured and fed,
nourished and cared for,
their whims indulged,
their exuberance encouraged.

May we be forced out of our
shroud of privilege and materialism to see
how things are so different
for children throughout the world.

Where the ravages of the earth prevent
access to good food and clean water;
where the ravages of war enforce a
nomadic existence and constant fear;
where the ravages of human failings lead
to neglect and abuse.
God, these too are your beloved children.

So help us to care,
to interfere
and to intervene
to live out our baptism promise,
to welcome and share God's love
with all God's children. Amen

Liz Crumlish, Spill the Beans

Pirate Jesus

A boss,
a spouse,
a parent,
a child –
there is always
someone
willing to hold my feet
to the fire;

and chaff:
there have been
a few
through the years
who have let me know
I'm part of that group
which should be swept up
and tossed aside;

but you come
to me,
dripping wet
with that dove
perched on your shoulder
(like a pirate
with his parrot)
and grabbing me
by the hand
you count, '1, 2, 3!'

and together
we jump
faith-first
into
grace.

Thom M Shuman

In this spirit we baptise you

This baby who is being presented to the assembly
is a moment of hope and joy.

We welcome him into this Christian community
not to determine his choice for him
but rather to educate him towards freedom.
If we succeed in this educational task of liberation
his person will be precious to us, whatever choices he makes;
we will be able to say that we have not suffocated your Spirit
who has given us this new gift of life.

The gesture of pouring water
expresses our awareness of being tied
to the great biblical events,
to all Christian tradition
and in particular to the baptism of Jesus in the Jordan.
As John stood before Jesus
we also place ourselves before this baby,
before all babies,
before all who are considered 'nothings' by the wise and powerful,
before those discriminated against,
before the least.

We also affirm that it is we who must be baptised:
it is also we who must pass through the water,
which is the sign of purification,
of liberation and of untiring struggle,
but finally of victory and resurrection.

In this spirit *(name of child)* we baptise you:
in the name of the Father, the Son and the Holy Spirit.

Part of a baptismal prayer prepared by members of Isolotto basic Christian Community, Italy.

Ian M Fraser

The baptism of Jesus 333

Look what you can be

Words and music by Roddy Cowie

Words and music © Roddy Cowie

334 Winter

Jesus said, 'Look what you can be:
you can be all that you see in me,
if you are born again of the Spirit
that soared over Jordan.'
Jesus said, 'Feel the Spirit blow:
give away everything; let go
safe in the circling power of the Spirit
that filled me in Jordan.
And beside that birth
all the rest is worth
straw in the fields after harvest.'

Jesus said, 'Bend to the Father's will
as the grass blows on a windy hill,
full of the life and grace of the Spirit
as I was in Jordan.'

Jesus said, 'What if it ends in death?
Give Him your praise with your latest breath;
enter the light and joy of the Spirit
as I did in Jordan.
And beside that birth
all the rest is worth
straw in the fields after harvest.'

Roddy Cowie

Prayers for Christian unity

An opening prayer

For the richness of your creation,
for different colours and scents,
for different birds and animals,
none the same, yet part of one creation,
Generous God,
We praise you.

For the richness of your world,
for different places and peoples,
for different songs and stories,
no person the same, yet part of one human family,
Generous God,
We praise you.

For the richness of our *town/city/village*,
for different families and homes,
for different places to work, play and learn,
no street the same, yet part of one community,
Generous God,
We praise you.

For the richness of our churches,
for different gifts and skills,
for different songs and prayers,
no congregation the same, yet part of one Church,
Generous God,
We praise you.

We praise you Lord for creating a world of wonder and beauty,
of diversity and difference.
You love and care for all that you have given
and long that your world should know peace.
Teach us, then, to live in harmony with you and our world:
Teach us to love, as you show love.
Amen

Simon Taylor

We ask for courage

We give thanks for your story, and we give thanks for our spiritual ancestors, who have lived and told your story faithfully through the generations.

Pause

We ask for courage as we receive your story: to live it well, and to tell it faithfully and appropriately in our time.

Pause

We give thanks for your abiding and transforming presence, and the myriad ways we encounter, experience and express relationship with you.

Pause

We ask for courage as we make space for the differences within the Christian community, and between those of Christian and other faith traditions.

Pause

We give thanks for the Spirit's gifts calling to each individual and congregation embodying Jesus in the world.

Pause

We ask for courage to celebrate difference, welcoming one another in love, as we rejoice with those who rejoice, and weep with those who weep.

Pause

We give thanks for Jesus the Christ, whom we follow on your way of Love.

Pause

We ask for courage to follow Jesus' call to love with radical hospitality, to live a different way, to be and to see him wherever we go.

Pause

In our words and our silence, Holy One, hear our prayers. Amen

Sarah Agnew

Our united service

Loving God, in the cold of January
we meet again in our united service.
This is the time when we get together
and meet our neighbours and friends
in a church that is not our own.

We come from several congregations and parishes
and meet to share worship, fellowship and food,
but more importantly to affirm that we are united.

We are not united organically,
nor in our understanding of church governance,
nor in our theology,
nor even in our regular observances.
But we are all united in our commitment
to try to follow Jesus of Nazareth:
who turned the world upside down
and continues to challenge us to change.

May we who journey together in this pilgrimage through life
open our hearts now to praise God,
the God of these winter days,
whose warm presence sings in our hearts
and makes us glad to be alive.

We pray that we may continue to be challenged
and continue to respond to the call of Jesus
so that the Kingdom may come in our lives
and in the world.

John Butterfield

Give us grace

As you, Father, are in me and I am in you, may they also be in us, so that the world may believe that you have sent me. (John 17:21)

(Tune: 'To God be the glory', CH4 512)

As Christ with the Father we're called to be one.
The Spirit close binding the Father and Son
invites into union all those who believe,
to die to themselves and new life to receive.

*Chorus: Give us grace, give us grace; what we are now to hold
as a gift for our times, your full purpose unfold,
and beckon us forward to die to the past
and rise to that union with you which will last.*

The world needs a sign to believe Jesus gave
the mind of the Father, creation to save;
accepting the state of our life here on earth
he yet brought the power to destroy sin and death.

Chorus

We love the familiar, the church ways we've known,
but God's will provides that which matters alone;
baptised into newness, by Eucharist fed,
we step to the future to which Christ has led.

Chorus

Ian M Fraser

Bidding prayers

God of wisdom and integrity,
you call your people to live together in joy and justice
and to celebrate the good news of your saving love.
Hear us now as we pray for our needs and the needs of the world.

We pray for those whose faces and stories
we have seen on the news this week:
for those who live in places of fear and war,
for those who are homeless,
for those whose decisions affect the lives of nations.
God, in your mercy,
Hear our prayer.

In this Week of Christian Unity
we ask you to help us to see clearly the divisions in our churches
and to be willing to engage in honest dialogue
with those whose ideas and traditions differ from our own.
God, in your mercy,
Hear our prayer.

We pray for the leaders of our churches.
We pray for our local community.
We pray that our churches may be faithful to your call to work together
and to share our resources with those in need.
God, in your mercy,
Hear our prayer.

We pray for those who are sick or sad or in trouble
and for those who care for them.
We pray for those who have died,
and their families and friends who love them and miss them.
God, in your mercy,
Hear our prayer.

We pray for our own needs, our hopes, our dreams.
God, in your mercy,
Hear our prayer.

Loving God,
you lead your children homewards.
Secure in our relationship with you
may we be reconciled with one another
and share your love and glory in the world.
Amen

Ruth Burgess

A prayer for Christian unity

Covenant God,
whose mission is to reconcile
and whose gift is peace,
teach us, we pray, to prefer
creation to destruction,
redemption to condemnation,
freedom to retaliation,
that in turning away from sinful division,
we may follow the path to new life
and renewed community.

Bless us as we seek
to fulfil your will and desire
to draw all things into unity with you,
our Maker, Saviour and Comforter,
now and for ever.

Terry Garley

Blessings and sendings

God's blessing be ours

God's blessing be ours:
a blessing of loving kindness,
a blessing of hope and courage,
a blessing of listening and love.
God's blessing be ours
always. Amen

Ruth Burgess

In our heart a dream

Let us go from here,
in our heart a dream
of a world without hatred
without anguish
without violence
without greed.

Let us go on the path of the dream
that the Kingdom is near
in today's world.
A dream which God has planted in us.
A dream which we must caress and pass on.

Let us dream that dream
and live that dream
and God will be with us.

Albert Klok

A winter blessing

May you find rest in the busyness,
stillness in the storm
and light in the darkness. Amen

Fiona van Wissen

A blessing from Bethlehem

This blessing is a rephrasing of a Christmas greeting sent in a card from Bethlehem by Hanna Azar, a Palestinian who had been a volunteer in Iona several times.

– Jan Sutch Pickard

May this coming year
be full of love, joy and peace,
in our hearts, in our communities
and in our countries;
may the small Jesus Baby born in Bethlehem
light our lives,
guide our ways toward the best
and save us from all harm.

Hanna Azar

A good work

May God,
who has begun a good work in us,
guard us and encourage us
and bless us on our journey,
and bring us at the last
surely and safely home. Amen

Ruth Burgess

May God salt the path before you

May God bless your winter days with warm sunshine and clear skies,
may God bless your winter nights with shining stars and a bright moon,
may God salt the path before you and light your way,
may God wrap you in his presence and warm you against winter cold.

Simon Taylor

When

When we are stretched thin, challenged and doubting,
We walk with God.

When we are in the midst of the life-giving, the exciting and the nourishing,
We walk with God.

When we question every decision and when we are truly certain,
We walk with God.

When we walk with hesitancy or dance with enthusiasm,
We walk with God.

Fiona Barker

Praying the day through

Tune: CM e.g. St Columba, St Fulbert

A prayer for rising from our beds,
for water, sponge and soap,
for clothes, for food, for family,
a prayer to help us cope.

A prayer for starting out the day,
for those who empty bins,
for those who sweep the streets and drive
the bus as day begins.

A prayer for those we walk beside,
for tasks to us assigned,
for getting home and time to rest,
work's worries left behind.

A prayer of thanks for shelter, warmth,
a prayer for those in want,
a prayer for those we love and hate,
then sleep in safety grant.

Ian M Fraser

Time for rest

May the snowflakes gently caress your face,
may the east wind not bite too deep,
may warm sunshine brighten winter days,
may the long nights give you time for rest
and may God warm you with the fire of his love.

Simon Taylor

Bless you

May God the Maker bless you:
God who speaks words of freedom and justice,
God who walks what he talks for ever.
May God bless you, with hope. **Amen**

May Jesus the teacher bless you:
Jesus who speaks of Good news for poor people,
Jesus who talks and does the business.
May Jesus bless you, with truth. **Amen**

May God the Holy Spirit bless you:
the Holy Spirit who speaks in fire and stillness,
the Holy Spirit who dances what she announces.
May the Holy Spirit bless you, with joy. **Amen**

Ruth Burgess

This long night

A blessing of the dark sky be yours,
of the white moon
and the faraway stars.

A blessing of the cold earth be yours,
of the hoarfrost
and the drifts of snow.

A blessing of a warm hearth be yours,
of a lighted fire
and a loving home.

A blessing of the Trinity be yours:
Maker,
Storyteller,
Holy Spirit,

this long night
and for evermore.

Ruth Burgess

Sources and acknowledgements

'Responses and prayers for the Sunday before Christmas', by Ruth Burgess, first published in *Expository Times*. Used by permission of Ruth Burgess

'Bring it all to me' – © Stephen Fischbacher and Suzanne Butler/Fischy Music 2014. From the CD *Bring It All to Me*, Fischy Music: www.fischy.com. Used by permission of Fischy Music

'Until the light comes again', by Andrew Foster, first published in *Friends and Enemies*, Ruth Burgess (Ed.), Wild Goose Publications, 2004

'Litany of the Christingle' – by Ruth Burgess and Sally Foster-Fulton, from the download 'Some Resources for a Christingle Service', Wild Goose Publications

'Are you ready?', by Sally Foster-Fulton, from *Hope Was Heard Singing*, by Sally Foster-Fulton, Wild Goose Publications, 2015

'He walked alone on Christmas Eve', by John Rackley, first published in the *Baptist Times*. Used by permission of John Rackley

'Christmas came simply', by Ruth Burgess, first published by Alternativity. Used by permission of Ruth Burgess

'As the old year passes', by David MacGregor © 2007 Willow Publishing. Used by permission of David MacGregor

'The "in between" Sunday', by Marjorie Dobson, published on www.theworshipcloud.com. Used by permission of Marjorie Dobson

'Angel in the dump', by Benjamin Pratt, from *Short Stuff from a Tall Guy*, by Benjamin Pratt, Read The Spirit Books, 2015. Used by permission of Benjamin Pratt

'In this spirit we baptise you', by members of Isolotto basic Christian Community, Italy, from *With Faith and Flair*, by Ian M Fraser

'An opening prayer', by Simon Taylor, originally published by Roots (CTBI) in January 2007 as part of a service for the Week of Prayer for Christian Unity. Used by permission of Simon Taylor

'We ask for courage', by Sarah Agnew, from sarahtellsstories.blogspot.com. Used by permission of Sarah Agnew

'Bless you', by Ruth Burgess, written for Church Action on Poverty, 2012. Used by permission of Ruth Burgess

Spill the Beans material © the contributors. Spill the Beans is 'a lectionary-based resource with a Scottish flavour for Sunday Schools, Junior Churches and worship leaders': http://spillbeans.org.uk/

About the authors

Sarah Agnew is a storyteller, poet and minister (Uniting Church in Australia), undertaking PhD studies in Biblical Literature and Oral Performance at the University of Edinburgh. Her poetry and prayers appear in several volumes, and on praythestory.blogspot.com and sarahtellsstories.blogspot.com.

Ruth Bamforth is a teacher and music educator for all ages, and has written children's songs for toddler and playgroups, CBeebies and Dunblane Cathedral Sunday Schools.

Fiona Barker is a primary-school teacher, working with four- and five-year-olds in Birmingham. She is also studying for an MA in Christian Spirituality, is a member of the Methodist Church and an associate of the Iona Community.

Stuart Barrie: Retired engineer, full-time dog-walker and zen bowler.

Elizabeth Baxter enjoys supporting individuals in their therapeutic and spiritual journeys at Holy Rood House in Thirsk, North Yorkshire, which she pioneered with her husband, Stanley, almost 25 years ago. Exploring theology through her priesthood, relationships, liturgy and poetry, Elizabeth seeks to make the connections and take the risks that will transform and heal individuals and communities, the church and the earth.

Keith Blackwood is in his 20th year as a minister in the Church of Scotland, is currently the minister of Mannofield Church in Aberdeen, and is a contributor to the Spill the Beans writing team.

Anna Bosatta lives with her husband in a small Hertfordshire village and considers herself privileged: it is a gift to have the freedom to explore spirituality and creativity of all sorts, and to share that life with family, local community and the broader church.

Ruth Bowen is a retired teacher who enjoys island life on Stronsay, one of the northern Orkney islands, where she likes to read, spin, weave, knit and garden, as well as join in island community events. Her husband, David, is also a retired teacher and a minister helping with services at the island kirk where they worship.

Ruth Burgess is a member of the Iona Community living in Dunblane. She enjoys being retired, writing and editing and growing fruit and vegetables. Her garden is graced by the antics of a murder of crows.

John Butterfield is the minister of Stromness Church of Scotland Parish Church, Orkney. He is a member of the Iona Community.

Elizabeth Clark is a Methodist minister who has spent fifteen years in rural ministry and is currently the National Rural Officer for the Methodist and United Reformed Churches. She is an Iona Community associate.

About the authors

David J.M. Coleman is a URC minister and digital artist, who has provided many images for Wild Goose Publications. His Facebook page, 'Lectionary Clips and Hymns', provides alternative visual reflections on the RCL readings shared by many churches.

Roddy Cowie is an Iona associate, a lay reader in the Church of Ireland and Emeritus Professor of Psychology at Queen's, Belfast. His academic work centred on efforts to let machines match some basic human abilities (mainly involving perception and emotion), and his current projects involve applying the lessons to issues like self-knowledge and a Christian understanding of emotion.

Kathy Crawford is a Reader in the Diocese of Southwell & Nottingham and a former foster carer. Her previously published work includes lots of resource material for under-five groups and all-age worship, plus several storybooks for young children. She now enjoys writing meditations and other resources for use in adult services.

Tricia Creamer is a member of Poole Methodists, and runs a weekly 'Celtic Colours' group at the church, exploring Christian spirituality through Celtic arts. She loves writing, teaching the piano, painting and being involved with projects which bring people together. She is an associate member of the Iona Community.

Liz Crumlish is a Church of Scotland minister living on the west coast of Scotland, coordinating a national church renewal project. A contributor to *Spill the Beans*, *Abingdon Creative Preachers Annual* and *There's a Woman in the Pulpit*, Liz is also a prolific blogger at www.liz-vicarofdibley.blogspot.com.

da Noust are members and friends of L'Arche Edinburgh, an ecumerical community of people with and without intellectual disabilities sharing life together to help create a more human society.

Judy Dinnen ministers and writes in Herefordshire. She loves Iona for its fresh approach to worship, its social awareness and, of course, its wonderful books.

Carol Dixon was born in Alnwick, Northumberland and is a lay preacher in the United Reformed Church and a Friend of St Cuthbert's, Lindisfarne, for whom she produced a CD of Holy Island hymns. Her prayers and hymns are in *Worship Live*, *HymnQuest*, *The URC Prayer Handbook* and *Church Hymnary 4*, the Church of Scotland hymnbook. She is a wife, mother and grandmother and enjoys touring with her husband in their Caravette.

Colin Dixon began writing music in his teens with his twin brother for their band in the local United Reformed Church. He enjoys playing rock/blues and works in farming in Northumberland and as a computer networking engineer.

Marjorie Dobson is well-known for her hymns, prayers and meditations, with her collection *Multi-coloured Maze* (Stainer & Bell) going into its second printing. She has been widely anthologised in the UK and abroad and has had several hymns included in the latest Methodist hymn book, *Singing the Faith*, as well as in other hymnals. She is a Methodist Local Preacher.

Fischy Music is a charity that supports the emotional, social and spiritual wellbeing of primary-age children: www.fischy.com.

Brian Ford: 'I am a retired sixth-form college biology teacher. I spend my time doing voluntary work, amateur dramatics, gardening and folk singing.'

Andrew Foster: An engineer, an elder in the Presbyterian Church in Canada, a frequent visitor to Iona and a contributor to a number of Wild Goose books.

Sally Foster-Fulton is the Head of Christian Aid Scotland and the author of several downloads and books, including *Hope Was Heard Singing: Resources for Advent*, Wild Goose Publications.

Ian M Fraser is a long-time member of the Iona Community, the author of many books and 'Margaret's man'. He is 99 years old.

Stuart Fulton is a parish minister in Stirling. He is originally from Northern Ireland and has lived and worked in Scotland, England and the United States.

Terry Garley: Education in Birmingham schools, at Leeds, Tübingen (Germany) and Nottingham universities and teaching experience in Derbyshire, Nottinghamshire and France (Agen & Lyon) developed my interest in language and literature. Becoming interested and involved in the ecumenical movement – locally, countywide and nationally – with some international experience in Dublin, Europe, North India and Southern Africa, each giving fresh insight into prayer, I remain influenced by this and by the Anglican collect as a form of expression of Christian faith and hope.

Liz Gibson is a member of the Iona Community and a Church of Scotland minister. She and Martyn live on a croft where, with the help of volunteers, they grow a variety of produce, including Isle of Mull Tea. She is passionate about the stewardship of the earth.

Nicky Gilbert is a self-supporting area minister living on Hayling Island on the south coast. She likes to paddle at low tide.

Louise Gough is a Methodist minister, currently serving at Trinity Methodist and United Reformed Church in Cheadle, Stockport. She enjoys preparing worship material for her congregation, playing the flute and relaxing with her huge cat, Wesley.

Liz Gregory-Smith lives with her husband in New Brancepeth, a village on the edge of Durham City. She is a retired teacher and is a Reader in the local Anglican church.

Roddy Hamilton is minister of New Kilpatrick Parish Church in Bearsden, having served just down the road in Clydebank. Both have been communities who have dared to explore faith imaginatively, poetically and with a plethora of questions – a creative combination.

Mary Hanrahan: 'I am a retired primary-school teacher, enjoying hobbies of card-making, a writing group and having fun with my two grandsons. An active parishioner of St Paul the Apostle Catholic Church, Shettleston, I am a minister of the Eucharist and member of the Bereavement group and book club.'

Marc Harshman, poet laureate of West Virginia, has seen his most recent full-length collection of poems, *Believe What You Can*, published by West Virginia University, and his thirteenth children's book, *One Big Family*, published by Eerdmans. Periodical publications include *The Georgia Review*, *Levure littéraire*, *Emerson Review*, *Anglican Theological Review* and *Poetry Salzburg Review*. He also was an invited reader at the Greenwich Book Festival in London in May 2016.

Pam Hathorn is a retired teacher who enjoys reading, looking at the heavens and longs to be wise.

Brian Hick is an Education Consultant and music critic who runs *Lark Reviews* (www.larkreviews.co.uk) and Lark Press. He is Editor Emeritus of *The Organ* and has published a wide range of verse, and histories of important pipe organs.

Sally Howell Johnson is a minister in the United Methodist Church in Minnesota, USA, is author of *The Practising Life: Simple Acts, Sacred Living* (Kirk House) and blogs at pause.hennepinchurch.org.

Jean Hudson: 'A retired Methodist minister, I live in Co. Durham with my husband, John, and our dog, Amy. Retirement has opened up time to spend with friends, photograph and reflect on signs of the seasons, write liturgies for my local church and learn to spin.'

Judith Jessop is a Methodist pioneer minister living on a large council estate in north Sheffield, offering a ministry of prayer and hospitality and relationship-building. She is also seeking to build community among people interested in spirituality and the Jesus story in Sheffield. Judith is an associate member of the Iona Community.

Peter Johnston is minister at Ferryhill Parish Church in Aberdeen, a keen musician, sometime blogger and editor of *Spill the Beans*.

Tina Kemp is a Church of Scotland auxiliary minister currently working as part of a team serving two congregations in the Helensburgh area of western Scotland. A former journalist, she writes for a number of worship publications, including *Pray Now* and *Spill the Beans*. She lives with Mhairi and in her spare time enjoys walking, swimming, kayaking and looking after her two pet tortoises.

Albert Klok is a minister in the Remonstrant Church, a church based on freedom and tolerance, at Meppel and Hoogeveen in the Netherlands: www.remonstranten.nl/engels/

S Anne Lawson is Vicar of the Cross Country Parishes of Acton, Church Minshull, Worleston and Wettenhall in South Cheshire. She is also Chaplain to the Cheshire Agricultural Society, which involves the privilege of chaplaincy at the Royal Cheshire Show in June each year. She shares her vicarage with two rescue cats: Solomon, a very large dark-brown-and-black Maine Coon cross, and Shadow, a small grey moggy. They are both large on personality and convinced that the sole purpose of the human race is to provide food on demand.

Pat Livingstone is a composer and music educator based in London. Recent pieces of work include 'Migration', for piano duo, and 'In the Gathering', for ukulele orchestra, flute, recorder and piano. http://soundcloud.com/pat-livingstone www.facebook.com/pat.livingstone.520, www.twitter.com/@PatLivingstone1

Jo Love is a Resource Worker with the Wild Goose Resource Group. Drawing others into creative thinkings and doings is her passion and delight.

Nikki Macdonald currently resides in the rural wilds of south Scotland, where she is learning the language of sheep and the rhythm of the turning seasons. A fan of ginger beer, good baking, the seaside, John Knox and Jesus – though not necessarily in that order – she occasionally thinks her life, as it turned out, was not quite what she imagined when growing up in tropical Queensland.

David MacGregor is a minister with the Uniting Church in Australia, living with his wife, Dale, in Brisbane, Queensland. He is a songwriter, passionate about worship and Christian education for all ages, and a Friend of the Iona Community.

Gordon MacLeod is a Scottish writer from the Isle of Arran, who now lives in Birkdale in Merseyside.

Rebeka Maples: 'I am a spiritual director, retired ordained minister and adjunct university professor, and continue to serve the church and university in interim capacity. In addition to academic publications, my writing focuses on the spiritual connections between nature and creation.'

Michael Marten is a member of the Iona Community. He is a photographer, theologian, historian and activist based in Stirlingshire. More of his photography is available at www.marten.scot.

June McAllister: a solitary in rural Galway with dogs, cats and hens.

Barbara Miller is a minister within the United Church of Canada and is blessed to serve in beautiful Northern Ontario, where she and her husband, Brent, also farm cattle. They have three grown children and two grandchildren.

Carolyn Morris: 'A long-time teacher and recently retired book creator and author, I am hoping to remain creative whilst coping with life-changing experiences.'

Jude Morton: Recently retired incumbent of All Saints, St Leonard's & St Ives, Ringwood. Now living in France and enjoying having time to spend with family and friends and hoping to do more writing.

Katie Munnik is a Canadian writer living in Cardiff. You can find her on Twitter @messy_table.

John Murning: 'I am currently minister at Sherwood Greenlaw Church in Paisley, and involved with *Spill the Beans*. I also serve as Club Chaplain with Airdrie Football Club. I previously served as minister in Denny Old, United Church of Bute, as an Army Chaplain, and as minister at New Cathcart. I am married to Linda and have two children, Sally and Jack.'

Katy Owen is a member of the Iona Community and an associate Church of Scotland minister.

Avis Palmer loves poetry and values silence. She is a Methodist Local Preacher in the Chester and Delamere Forest Circuit, who believes in prompting insight through imagination.

Sarah Pascoe: ex-nurse, mother and grandmother, who loves to live by the sea.

Teri Carol Peterson is a pastor in the Presbyterian Church (USA). She is co-author of *Who's Got Time: Spirituality for a Busy Generation* (Chalice 2013), blogs at CleverTitleHere.blogspot.com, and enjoys reading, travelling and creating new ways for people to encounter God in worship.

Chris Polhill is a member of the Iona Community, and one of the first women to be ordained priest in the Church of England. Chris and her husband, John, run the Reflection Gardens on the edge of Cannock Chase: www.reflectiongardens.org.uk.

Benjamin Pratt is a United Methodist minister who worked for many years as a pastoral counsellor. He is an advocate for caregivers and an author. His books include *A Guide for Caregivers* and *Short Stuff from the Tall Guy: Lenten Meditations on Seeking Peace in a Troubled World*. Benjamin lives near Washington DC with his wife, Judith.

John Rackley lives in Leicestershire.

Julie Rennick is a Church of Scotland minister serving a rural community in the Scottish borders. She is a regular contributor to Spill the Beans and to RevGalBlogPals (revgalblogpals.org). Her own blog is 'A Country Girl' (http://julie-acountrygirl.blogspot.co.uk), which contains sermons and reflections.

Katherine Rennie is a retired solicitor and mediator and is a Local Preacher with the Methodist Church. She is a member of the Iona Community.

Joan Reppert is a spouse, mom, grandmom, published composer/arranger and piano teacher, who lives in Ithaca, New York. Joan and Nelson have lovely memories of their six weeks as 'vollies' on Iona as a celebration of Nelson's retirement from 50 years of ministry in the United Methodist Church.

Sue Sabbagh has written poetry since childhood. A few poems have appeared in print or been used on BBC radio. Her main work has been as a wife and mother, but she has also done some journalism and bereavement counseling, and has a degree in English Literature from Girton College, Cambridge and a Certificate in Religious Studies from Birkbeck, University of London.

Anne Seymour worked as a medic during the civil war in Nigeria, from where she was deported, in North Tyneside A and E, and in Cameroon. She retired in 1996. In 2015 she was awarded an MBE for her services to asylum seekers and refugees in the borough of South Tyneside. Anne died in August 2016.

Norman Shanks is a former Leader of the Iona Community.

Robert Shooter: 'My English teacher confiscated my jotter because he rightly felt I was writing stuff other than that he had set in class. I thought I'd never see it again, but at the next lesson I did, as he said. 'Why don't you write like that for me?' and I've been trying ever since.'

Thom M Shuman serves as a semi-retired pastor. Committed to non-violence, he supports justice for immigrants, refugees and people with mental illness. He is an associate of the Iona Community, and the author of several books and downloads, including *The Soft Petals of Grace*, Wild Goose Publications.

Peter Siney: Originally from the North West of England, Peter now works in Pastoral Ministry in Dublin, Ireland.

Jan Sutch Pickard is a poet, preacher and storyteller living in Mull. She worked in the Iona Community's centres on Iona for six years, and served with EAPPI in the West Bank.

Evelyn Sweerts is an associate member of the Iona Community, Church of England Ordinand, and wife and mother. When she's not busy herding children, she likes to bake and read, though rarely at the same time.

Kira Taylor is in her second year of A-levels and is hoping to study journalism at university, with a view to raising awareness of social inequalities through ethical reporting. Her poem here reflects her time struggling with ME and God's guidance through it.

Simon Taylor is a Baptist minister and chaplain living and working in Exeter. He enjoys writing liturgies and prayers, particularly inspired by the natural world or the life of Jesus. He also aims to bake a loaf of bread at least weekly.

Bonnie Thurston resigned a professorship and chair in New Testament to live quietly in her home state of West Virginia. Author of academic works, books on spirituality and five small collections of poetry, she works in a food pantry in Wheeling, WV, USA.

Margery Toller is a mother and grandmother who finds birth miraculous and knows how crucial a loving community is for everyone when they are born. She has worked as a chaplain in a hospital, prison and hospice.

Reinhild Traitler-Espiritu worked with the WCC before she became Director of the Protestant Academy Boldern near Zurich. She just retired from being President of the Interreligious Conference of European Women Theologians (IKETH), to have more time for writing and her intercontinental family.

Fiona van Wissen: 'I am currently involved with programmes and environmental projects at Crieff Hills Retreat and Conference Centre near Guelph, Ontario. I am most grateful to people I met while volunteering on Iona and friends at L'Arche for inspiring my writing.'

Zam Walker (1962-2016) was a worker with Women's Aid, a URC minister and a member of the Iona Community. She is much missed by David, Talie and Millie, and by the wonderful supportive family the Iona Community has become for us.

Pamela Whyman: 'I am a retired teacher, using the freedom retirement gives to enjoy hobbies, particularly gardening and tatting. I'm a volunteer with Restore, a Birmingham Churches Together project supporting asylum seekers and refugees.'

Jenny Wilson was born in England and is an Anglican priest in Adelaide, South Australia. She is Canon Precentor of St Peter's Cathedral, where she loves working with the stories of scripture and those of her community and singing with the Cathedral Choir. Jenny lectures in Homiletics at St Barnabas Theological College, North Adelaide.

Greta Wrigley lives in Leicester and writes hymns and songs. She retired five years ago and is involved in her local church.

Wild Goose Publications, the publishing house of the Iona Community established in the Celtic Christian tradition of Saint Columba, produces books, e-books, CDs and digital downloads on:

- holistic spirituality
- social justice
- political and peace issues
- healing
- innovative approaches to worship
- song in worship, including the work of the Wild Goose Resource Group
- material for meditation and reflection

Visit our website at
www.ionabooks.com
for details of all our products and online sales